Newnes AutoCAD® Pocket Book

For Dave & Joe

Newnes AutoCAD® Pocket Book

Peter Ingham

NEWNES

Newnes
An imprint of Butterworth-Heinemann Ltd
Linacre House, Jordan Hill, Oxford OX2 8DP

A member of the Reed Elsevier group

OXFORD LONDON BOSTON
MUNICH NEW DELHI SINGAPORE SYDNEY
TOKYO TORONTO WELLINGTON

First published 1993

British Library Cataloguing in Publication Data
A catalogue record for this book is available from the British Library

ISBN 0 7506 0807 2

Printed in England by Clays Ltd, St Ives plc

Contents

(Commands in boldface are Release 12 only)

Preface xiii

1 Using AutoCAD

The Screen Layout 1
The Main Screen Menu 2
Pull-down Menus 2
Dialogue Boxes 3
Tablet Input 5
Special Keys 5
Transparent Commands 6
Finding Commands 6
Coordinates 8
Limits & Extents 10

2 Drawing Commands

ARC 11
BPOLY 12
CHAMFER 13
CIRCLE 14
DLINE 15
DONUT 16
DOUGHNUT 16
ELLIPSE 17
FILLET 18
LINE 18
PLINE 19
POINT 21
POLYGON 22
RECTANG 22
SKETCH 23
SOLID 24
TRACE 24

3 Editing Commands

ALIGN 26
ARRAY 26
BREAK 28
CHANGE 29
CHPROP 30
COLOR 30
COPY 31
DDCHPROP 32
DDGRIPS 33

DDMODIFY 34
DDSELECT 35
DIVIDE 36
ERASE 37
EXPLODE 38
EXTEND 38
FILL 39
MEASURE 39
MIRROR 40
MOVE 41
OFFSET 41
OOPS 42
PEDIT 43
REDO 44
ROTATE 45
SCALE 46
SELECT 46
STRETCH 48
TRIM 49
U 50
UNDO 50

4 Display Controls

APERTURE 52
BLIPMODE 52
DDUCS 52
DDVIEW 63
DRAGMODE 53
DVIEW 54
GRAPHSCR 56
MENU 56
MSPACE 57
MVIEW 57
PAN 58
PLAN 59
PSPACE 59
REDRAW 60
REDRAWALL 60
REGEN 60
REGENALL 60
REGENAUTO 61
TEXTSCR 61
UCS 62
UCSICON 63
VIEW 63
VIEWPORTS 65

VPOINT 64
VPORTS 65
ZOOM 66

5 Annotation & Hatching

ASCTEXT 68
BHATCH 69
DDEDIT 72
DTEXT 72
HATCH 74
LINETYPE 76
LTSCALE 77
QTEXT 78
STYLE 78
TEXT 79

6 Dimensioning

DDIM 82
DIM 83
DIM: ALigned 84
ANgular 85
Baseline 86
CEntre 87
COntinue 87
Diameter 88
Exit 89
HOMetext 89
HORizontal 89
Leader 90
Newtext 91
OBlique 91
ORdinate 92
OVerride 93
RAdius 93
REDraw 94
REStore 95
ROtated 95
SAve 96
STAtus 97
STYle 97
TEdit 97
TRotate 98
UNdo 98
UPdate 98

VARiables 99
VERtical 99
DIM1 100

7 Working in 3D

3D 101
3DARRAY 102
3DFACE 103
3DMESH 104
3DPOLY 105
DDSOLMASSP 105
DDSOLVAR 106
EDGESURF 106
ELEV 108
FINISH 108
HIDE 111
ISOPLANE 111
LIGHT 112
MIRROR3D 113
PEDIT(3D) 115
PFACE 116
RENDER 116
RENDSCR 117
REPLAY 117
REVSURF 118
ROTATE3D 119
RPREF 119
RULESURF 121
SCENE 121
SHADE 122
SOLAREA 123
SOLCHP 123
SOLDISP 124
SOLFEAT 124
SOLIDIFY 125
SOLINT 126
SOLLIST 126
SOLMASSP 127
SOLMESH 127
SOLMOVE 128
SOLPURGE 129
SOLSEP 129
SOLSUB 130
SOLUCS 130
SOLUNION 131
SOLVAR 131

SOLWIRE 132
STATS 132
TABSURF 133

8 Blocks & Attributes
ATTDEF 134
ATTDISP 135
ATTEDIT 135
ATTEXT 136
BASE 137
BLOCK 138
DDATTDEF 139
DDATTE 140
DDATTEXT 140
DDINSERT 141
INSERT 142
MINSERT 144
SHAPE 145
WBLOCK 146
XBIND 146
XREF 147

9 Plotting & Files
APPLOAD 150
COMPILE 151
DDVIEW 151
DXBIN 152
DXFIN 152
DXFOUT 153
FILES 154
GIFIN 156
IGESIN 157
IGESOUT 157
LOAD 158
NEW 158
OPEN 159
PCXIN 160
PLOT 160
PSDRAG 162
PSFILL 162
PSIN 163
PSOUT 163
PSQUALITY 164
QSAVE 165
RCONFIG 165
SAVE 166

SAVEAS 167
SAVEIMG 167
TIFIN 156

10 The Drawing Environment

ABOUT 169
CONFIG 169
DDEMODES 170
DDLMODES 171
DDOSNAP 172
DDRENAME 173
DDRMODES 174
DDUNITS 175
END 177
FILTER 177
GRID 179
HANDLES 179
LAYER 180
LIMITS 181
MULTIPLE 182
MVSETUP 182
ORTHO 184
OSNAP 184
QUIT 186
REDEFINE 186
REINIT 186
RENAME 187
SETVAR 187
SNAP 188
TABLET 189
UNDEFINE 190
UNITS 191
VIEWRES 192
VPLAYER 192

11 Miscellaneous

AREA 193
AUDIT 194
CAL 194
DBLIST 195
DELAY 195
DIST 196
FILMROLL 196
HELP 197
ID 198
LIST 198

MSLIDE 199
PURGE 199
RESUME 200
RSCRIPT 200
SCRIPT 201
SH 202
SHELL 202
STATUS 202
TIME 203
TREESTAT 203
VSLIDE 204

12 System Variables 205

I am grateful to the staff of Autodesk (UK) Ltd whom I found to be most helpful and encouraging.

PREFACE

AutoCAD Release 12 contains many improvements. It is faster, is easier to use and contains many new facilities.

Its improved speed is due to several factors. A larger 32-bit virtual screen means less frequent and quicker regenerations. The file handling is now quicker. The hidden-line removal algorithm has been improved so that producing drawings of solid models is much faster.

The provision of many extra dialogue boxes means that the more complicated commands may be carried out much more conveniently. The new context-sensitive HELP facility can give detailed assistance precisely when it is required. The object grabs facility allows the more common editing operations to be performed without any explicit commands at all. Hatching and plotting may be carried out more predictably because of previews being provided.

Many new commands have been included - those with boldface text in the list of contents - and many of the old commands have been revamped to improve their capability and ease of use. Rendering may now be carried out without having to buy another system. Bitmapped images may be imported and exported in the commoner formats. The SQL extension permits communication with external databases.

Because of these and other improvements and additions, AutoCAD is now larger than ever and this results in a larger manual which is fine for reference but inconvenient in normal use. This pocket book should be invaluable both to experienced users and beginners. It is organised in a broadly functional manner, commands being grouped by their actions into sections.

For experienced AutoCAD users:

If you know the name of a command and want to find out how it works in Release 12, locate it in the command index in the list of contents on Page i. Commands new in Release 12 are shown in boldface type. The explanation given in the body of the Pocket Book includes details of the operation of the command and how the command can be located in the AutoCAD menu maze.

For less experienced users:

If you are completely new to AutoCAD and want to find out how it is organised → **Section 1**

If you want to perform some operation and suspect that there is a command that will be suitable:

- If you want to draw lines on the drawing → **Section 2**
- If you want to alter lines you have made → **Section 3**
- If you want to change the way your drawing is shown on the screen → **Section 4**
- If you want to add text to your drawing → **Section 5**
- If you want to hatch shapes on your drawing → **Section 5**
- If you want to add dimensions → **Section 6**
- If you want to draw 3D shapes → **Section 7**
- If you want to add predefined elements to your drawing → **Section 8**
- If you want to plot a drawing on paper → **Section 9**
- If you want to read or write to a computer file → **Section 9**
- If you want drawing aids → **Section 10**
- If you want a list of system variables → **Section 12**
- If you want a complete list of commands → **Section 13**
- If none of the above describes your needs → **Section 11**

The AutoCAD Pocket Book contains explanations of the standard commands and also of the more useful AutoLISP programs supplied with the system.

Peter Ingham
Summer 1993

1 Using AutoCAD

The Screen Layout

The drawing editor screen has four areas.

The Status Line is a strip at the top of the screen which is used as a reminder of drawing mode settings. It shows the name of the current layer, the word "Snap" if SNAP mode is ON, the word "Ortho" if ORTHO mode is ON, the word "Tablet" if tablet mode is ON and the letter "P" if Paperspace is in force. On the right hand side of the status line, the cursor crosshair's positional coordinates may be displayed.

The Main Screen Menu is a vertical strip down the right side of the screen. It contains a list of items that may be selected by picking with the pointing device. Each item in the list is highlighted as the pointing device is moved to cover it.

The Prompt Area is a horizontal strip along the bottom of the screen. This is used for communication with the system. Commands typed on the keyboard are echoed here. Prompts and error messages from the drawing editor are displayed also.

The Drafting Area is the rectangular space in which the drawing is displayed.

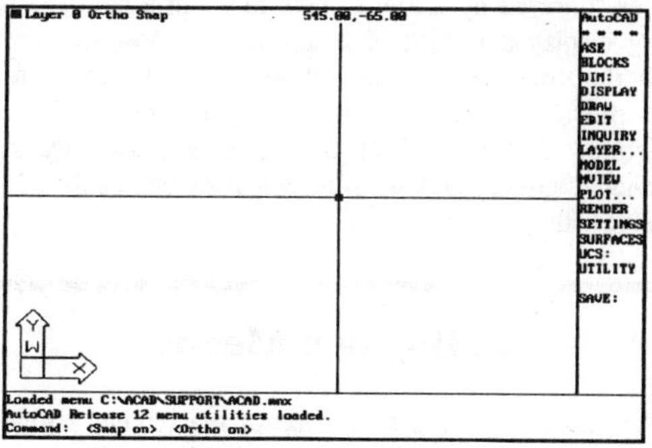

1.1 The Screen Layout

The Main Screen Menu

When the drawing editor is entered, a menu holding several items is displayed. Since the space is far too small to hold all the AutoCAD commands, each of the menu items is a functional group - for instance, Draw. If one of these items is picked, another menu holding all the items in the group appears. The process may be repeated. This means that the menu structure of AutoCAD is tree-like and the first menu displayed is known as the "Root Menu".

AutoCAD provides a standard menu, details of which are held in the file ACAD.MNU and its compiled form in the file ACAD.MNX. The standard menu holds 17 items. In further menu pages, if the word "AutoCAD" at the top of a menu is clicked, a return is made to the root menu. Another item on the menu is a row of stars. If this is clicked, a list of object snaps appears. This may be used as an aid to selecting entities. For example, if Center is picked, then a circle selected, the point returned to the system is the centre of that circle. Some other useful commands are also held in this group.

Often, the number of items in a menu group is too large for the space available. An item next is provided and if this is picked, the remaining items in the group are displayed. Item names followed by a colon are AutoCAD commands. Item names followed by a row of dots result in a dialogue box being displayed instead of a sub-menu. Most sub-menus have the three items: Last, Draw and Edit at their foot. Last provides a very convenient way of back in the menu structure. Draw and Edit are the most commonly used command groups and their menus may be displayed by picking either of them.

Pull Down Menus

If the cursor is moved to the top of the screen, a row of options appears instead of the status line. The cursor changes from a crosshair to an arrow. The horizontal row of items is similar in function to the side menu although the items listed are different and the menu acts in a different way.

If one of the options in the list is picked, a vertical menu appears. This is called a "pull down menu". A triangular mark follows some menu items. If the cursor is moved over one of these, a sub-menu appears to the right. This is called a "cascading menu". The pull down menu may be exited by clicking outside the menu area.

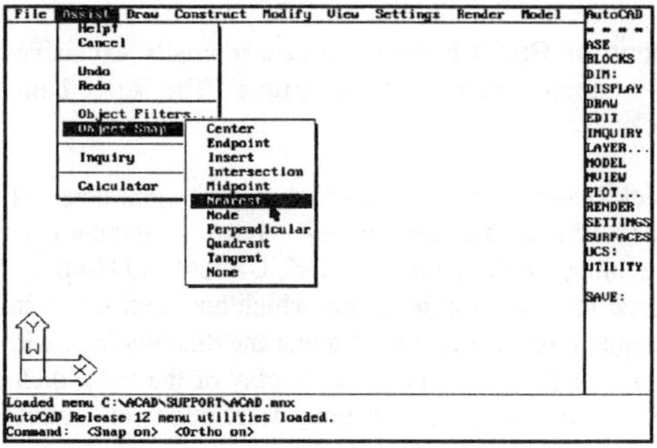

1.2 Pull-down Menus

Dialogue Boxes

Some commands, and all those with names starting with "DD", result in the display of a dialogue box. When the dialogue box appears, the cursor changes into an arrow. Options are picked by typing in special areas in the dialogue box and by clicking on named buttons. All other methods of communicating with the system, picking entities, typing commands and picking menu items are disabled while the dialogue box is being displayed. This procedure should be familiar to any Microsoft Windows user and is particularly useful for some of the more complex commands. The options in a dialogue box are partitioned into logical areas or groups, each group being outlined and given an explanatory name. There are several types of input area in a dialogue box. Movement from button to button is conveniently done using the pointing device but it is possible to use the TAB key to jump from one to another.

Action Buttons, when clicked, make some kind of process take place. The button's name may be followed by three dots. When such a button is clicked, another dialogue box appears. The button's name may be followed by "<". If this type of button is clicked, the dialogue box is temporarily cleared from the screen so that some action requiring the whole drawing area may be done. An example is the selection of entities for modifying. Some buttons are more heavily outlined than others. These are default settings which may be activated by typing RETURN. Any button that is currently unavailable is shown greyed out.

Option or Radio buttons are in a mutually exclusive set. Only one may be activated at a time. The active button is blacked in.

Check buttons are in groups that may be simultaneously in force. Most dialogue boxes have a standard group containing the three buttons: OK, Cancel and Help.... OK is used for applying the action which has been set up in the dialogue box, Cancel for leaving the dialogue box with no action. Help... results in the display of the Help dialogue box which gives an on-line description of AutoCAD commands and their actions.

List boxes contain sets of items such as file names. Elements of the list are selected by clicking the required name. If appropriate, more than one item may be selected by holding down the SHIFT key when clicking names. Often, there are too many items to show in the space available and just a few are displayed, the rest being viewed by using a scroll bar. Similar to List boxes are Pop-up lists. These contain a scrollable list of options.

Text input boxes are used for names entered from the keyboard. When a text input box is clicked, a small vertical cursor appears. This, in conjunction with the normal arrow keys, backspace, delete and insert keys, may be used to edit names. When the text input box is double-clicked, all existing text is highlighted. It may then be replaced by new text. A typical dialogue box is shown in Figure 1.3.

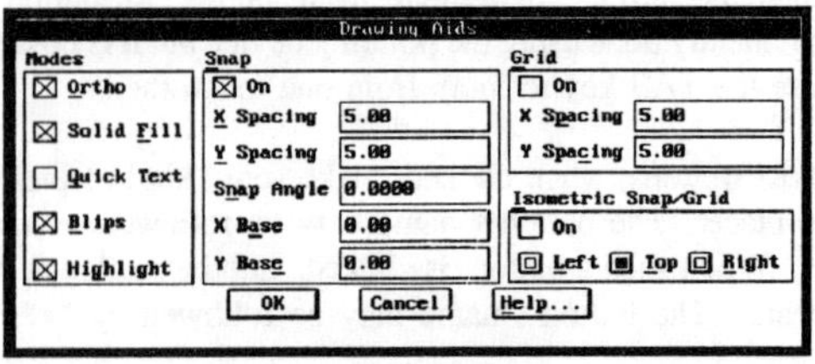

1.3 Dialogue Boxes

Tablet Input

An alternative way of driving AutoCad is to use a digitising tablet and some type of pointing device such as a puck or a stylus. A tablet overlay is fixed securely to the flat surface of the digitising tablet, and the tablet is calibrated so that the system knows the overlay's position. On the overlay, certain areas are dedicated to AutoCAD commands and pointing to and clicking these areas results in the command being activated. If a multi-button pointing device is used, the buttons may be allocated to common operations such as turning snap mode on. Usually, a rectangular section of the overlay is reserved for drawing.

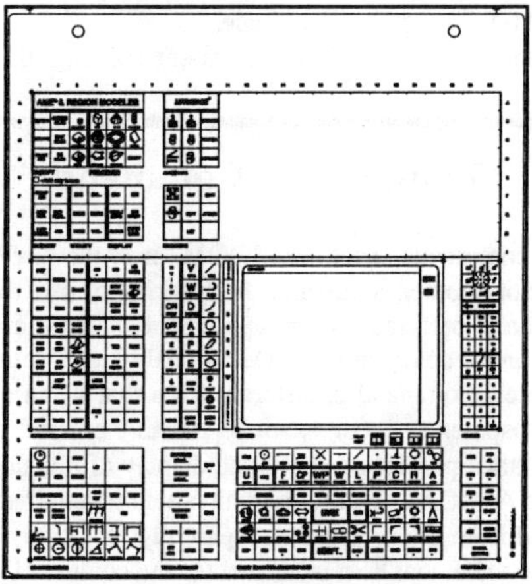

1.4 Standard AutoCAD Template

Templates may be customised quite easily for particular applications and many are part of the wide range of specialised systems which use AutoCAD as a vehicle. AutoCAD provides its own standard template - see Figure 1.4.

Special Keys

Usually, six function keys are allocated special functions.

F1 toggles the display between graphics and text.

F6	toggles coordinate display on the status line.
F7	toggles display of grid.
F8	toggles ORTHO mode.
F9	toggles SNAP mode.
F10	toggles tablet mode.

Some actions may be performed by holding down the CONTROL key and hitting a letter key.

Ctrl-B	toggles SNAP mode.
Ctrl-C	cancels current command.
Ctrl-D	toggles coordinate display.
Ctrl-G	toggles grid display.
Ctrl-O	toggles ORTHO mode.
Ctrl-Q	toggles output redirection to printer.
Ctrl-T	toggles tablet mode.
Ctrl-X	cancels all characters entered on a line.

Transparent Commands

Some commands, such as ZOOM, may be used in the middle of another command. In this kind of use, they must be entered prefixed by an apostrophe. They are called "transparent commands". Occasionally, the action of a transparent command is different from that when it is used non-transparently. For example, HELP, entered after the Command: prompt results in the display of a dialogue box and the AutoCAD feature for which help is required may be selected from a list. Used transparently, 'HELP is sensibly taken to mean that help is needed for the command in which it is embedded.

Finding Commands

For the experienced user, a strength of AutoCAD is the variety of ways in which commands may be entered. For instance, the command SNAP may be entered by;

- Typing Ctrl-B to toggle SNAP
- Hitting the function key F9 to toggle SNAP
- Typing SNAP at the Command: prompt

- Picking SETTINGS, then next, then SNAP: from the side menu

- Pulling down the Settings menu, then picking Drawing Aids.... Snap mode may then be entered from the dialogue box.

- Pointing to SNAP on a tablet overlay if one is available

A result of this variety is that over a period users can evolve a method of working which suits them best. They often use a mixture of typing and menu picking to achieve the most efficient way of drafting.

Unfortunately, the various ways of invoking commands is rather bewildering to the new user. It is often difficult to locate a command in the menu trees. In the sections which follow, the alternative methods of entering a command are shown as follows:

- Command: **SNAP** means that the command may be typed and echoed in the prompt area in response to the Command: prompt.

- **→ SETTINGS → next → SNAP:** means that SETTINGS and its subsequent options are picked from the side menu.

- **↓ Settings → Drawing Aids...** means that the Settings menu is pulled down from the top of the screen and Drawing Aids... picked from it.

It is unnecessary to type in the whole option name. Usually the first letter is sufficient; this is generally shown on the option list in upper case. Occasionally, more than one option will have the same initial letter and in this case, two letters, which are capitalised, are sufficient. An example is the PLINE options list:

Angle/CEnter/CLose/Direction/Halfwidth/Line/
Radius/Second pt/Undo/Width/<Endpoint of arc>:

Angle may be selected by typing A. CEnter may be selected by typing CE because CLose has the same initial letter.

Coordinates

The basic coordinate system in AutoCAD is called the World Coordinate System (or WCS). It cannot be changed. It is often more convenient to work with a local coordinate system with origin displaced from that of the WCS and with ordinates rotated with respect to those of the WCS. This is called the User Coordinate System (or UCS). The two coordinates systems are often coincident.

So that there will be no confusion over which coordinate system is in force, the display provides an icon showing the positive X and Y directions. A box appears at the bottom of the icon if the positive Z direction is pointing out of the display.

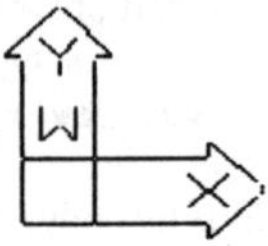

1.5 Icons (a)

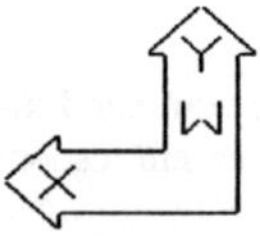

1.6 Icons (b)

If there is no box, the positive Z direction is pointing into the display. If the current UCS and WCS are coincident, a W is displayed in the icon.

If the icon is placed at the origin of the current UCS, a + is placed inside the box.

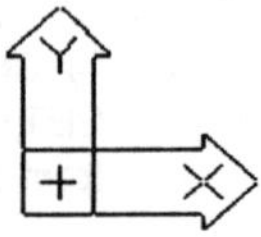

1.7 Icons (c)

1.8 Icons (d)

If the drawing is being viewed along the X-Y plane of the UCS or within one degree of it, the normal icon is replaced by a box containing a broken pencil.

AutoCAD provides two ways of working - in Modelspace and Paperspace. The drawing is often done in Modelspace while various views of the model may be constructed in Paperspace. When in Paperspace, the UCS icon arrows are replaced by a triangle.

1.9 Icons (e)

Coordinates may be supplied to the system in various ways:

- Absolute Cartesian coordinates are supplied by typing numbers separated by commas.

  1.234,-2.345 is a 2D coordinate

  1.234,-2.345,4.50 is a 3D coordinate

  These define points relative to the origin of the current UCS. If no Z-coordinate is supplied, the Z is assumed to be the current elevation, set by using the ELEV command. From Release 11, fractions may be input directly; 5-1/4 being the same as 5.25.
- Relative Cartesian coordinates are prefixed by the character @. These define points relative to the previous point defined. A special case is @ on its own, which is taken to mean the same coordinates as those of the previous point defined.
- Absolute polar coordinates in 2D are supplied by typing the distance from the UCS origin then a < symbol followed by the angle from the UCS origin in the X-Y plane: 1.234<45. Relative coordinates are again prefixed by @.
- Polar coordinates in 3D may be in one of two forms: spherical or cylindrical. The spherical form is supplied by typing the distance from the UCS origin followed by the angle in the X-Y plane followed by the angle from the X-Y plane, separated by < symbols: 1.234<45<30. The cylindrical form is supplied by typing the distance from the UCS origin followed by the angle in the X-Y plane followed by the Z-coordinate. The separators are a comma and a < symbol: 1.234<45,2.345. Relative coordinates are prefixed by @.
- Coordinates relative to the WCS - world coordinates - are prefixed by an asterisk: *1.234,2.345. Relative coordinates, world coordinates and polar coordinates may be combined: @*1.234<45.

Limits and Extents

AutoCAD holds details of the drawing in a virtual screen. The drawing is displayed through a window into this virtual screen. The part of the drawing displayed on the screen may be moved around by panning and may be scaled by zooming. If these operations produce displays outside the virtual screen, the coordinates of each displayed object must be recalculated. This process is called regeneration. For a large drawing, this takes up a long (sometimes irritatingly long) time.

Although AutoCAD can cope with very large drawings, it is often necessary to restrict drawing to a defined rectangle. These Limits are set by defining a rectangular area within which drawing is to be done. If an attempt is made to draw outside limits, a warning message appears. Limit checking may be turned on and off.

Another bounded window in the drawing is called its extents. This is the largest area that can be displayed showing all the entities on the drawing.

When zooming into or out of a drawing, several options are available. Two of these are Extents and All. If the Extents option is chosen, the zoom is made so that all the objects on the drawing are shown on the display as large as possible. If All is chosen, the zoom is to extents or limits, whichever is the larger.

2 Drawing Commands

ARC
- draws circular arcs

Command Sequence

Command: **ARC**
→ **DRAW** → **ARC**
↓ **Draw** → **Arc▸**

Command Options

The first prompt issued is: Center/<Start point>:. The default definition of an arc is by specifying three non-collinear points. In other options, the order of definition is important. The other methods of definition are:

- Start, centre, endpoint (SCE): define start point, type C, define the centre, define the endpoint.
- Start, centre, included angle (SCA): define start point, type C, define the centre, type A, enter angle.
- Start, centre, chord length (SCL): define start point, type C, define centre, type L, enter length of chord.
- Start, endpoint, radius (SER): define start point, type E, define endpoint, type R, enter radius.
- Start, endpoint, included angle (SEA): define start point, type E, define endpoint, type A, enter angle.
- Start, endpoint, starting direction (SED): define start point, type E, define endpoint, enter direction of arc.

The positive direction for arcs is anticlockwise. Where there are two possible arcs, a positive length, radius or angle results in the minor arc being drawn, negative values give the major arc.

The start direction is often most conveniently defined by picking a point. An arc which continues smoothly from a previously drawn line or arc may be obtained by entering RETURN in response to the prompt for start point. The arc is then fully defined when another point is specified. The system variable LASTANG holds the final tangent angle for the last arc drawn. If DRAGMODE is ON, the arc is displayed dynamically while it is being defined.

BPOLY*

- creates a polyline outlining entities

Command Sequence

Command: **BPOLY**

Command Options

The Polyline Creation dialogue box is displayed.

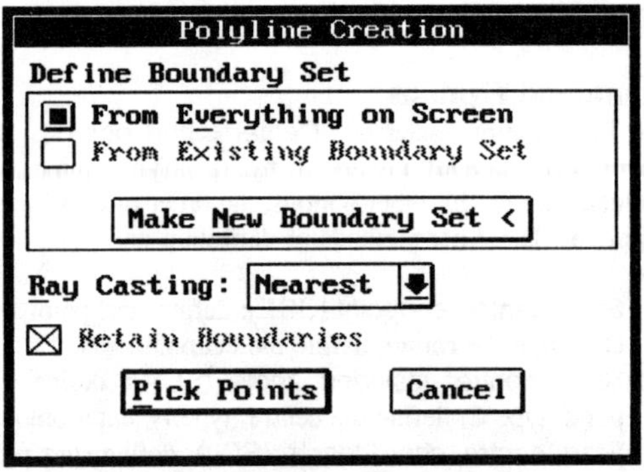

2.1 Polyline Creation Dialogue Box

- Define Boundary Set. This is a group of options determining the method of selecting entities. The Make New Boundary Set button enables the selection of displayed entities. The From Existing Boundary Set button enables entities already selected to be considered. The From Everything on Screen button results in all displayed entities being considered.
- Ray Casting. This is a pop-up list which specifies in which direction the system is to search for a boundary. The options are: Nearest, -X, +X, -Y and +Y. For example, if Nearest is in force, the boundary is sought starting with the entity closest to the point picked.
- Retain Boundaries. This is a check box which controls the creation of a closed polyline from the calculated boundary.
- Pick Points. This enables the picking of displayed points specifying the area from which the polyline will be constructed.

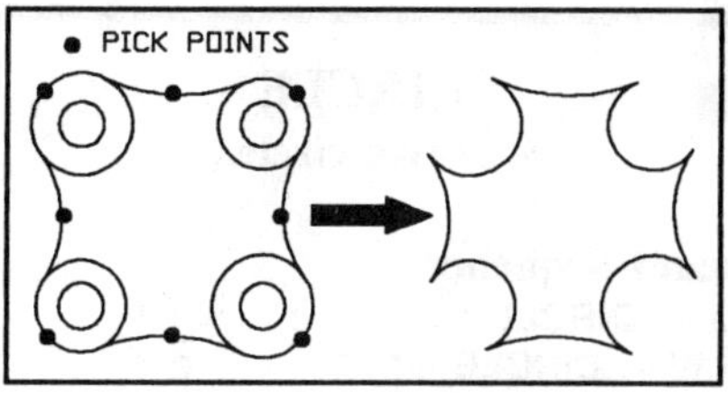

2.3 BPOLY Command

CHAMFER

- adds a chamfer to two lines

Command Sequence

Command: **CHAMFER**
→ **EDIT** → **CHAMFER:**
↓ **Construct** → **Chamfer**

Command Options

The prompt: Polyline/Distances/<Select first line>: is issued. The default option is to pick the two lines for chamfering. If different trim distances have been specified, the order of selection is significant.

The two lines do not need to intersect - the operation can be considered as extending them to their intersection point before chamfering. Also, the lines do not need to finish at their intersection point. In this case, they will be trimmed back to the point of intersection before chamfering, the trimming being carried out on the line segments on the side of the intersection point opposite from the pick positions.

Distances option sets trim distances for subsequent chamfering operations. Polyline option permits all suitable intersections of a polyline to be picked in one operation.

The system variables CHAMFERA holds the first chamfer distance which corresponds to the first line picked and CHAMFERB holds the second distance corresponding to the second line picked.

CIRCLE
- draws circles

Command Sequence
Command: **CIRCLE**
→ **DRAW** → **CIRCLE**
↓ **Draw** → **Circle▸**

Command Options
The first prompt is 3P/2P/TTR/<Center point>:. The five methods of definition are:

- Centre and radius: the centre is defined, then the radius. This is the default method.
- Centre and diameter: the centre is defined, D typed, then the diameter entered.
- Two endpoints of a diameter: 2P is typed, then the two points are defined.
- Three points on the circumference: 3P is typed, then the three points defined.
- Two tangents and a radius: TTR is entered, the two tangents specified then the radius. A tangent may be specified by selecting an existing line, circle or arc.

The TTR option often leads to an ambiguous definition - see Figure 2.4. AutoCAD resolves this by assuming that the positions of the pick points are hints as to which of the possible circles is intended. This means that the position of the pick point is significant.

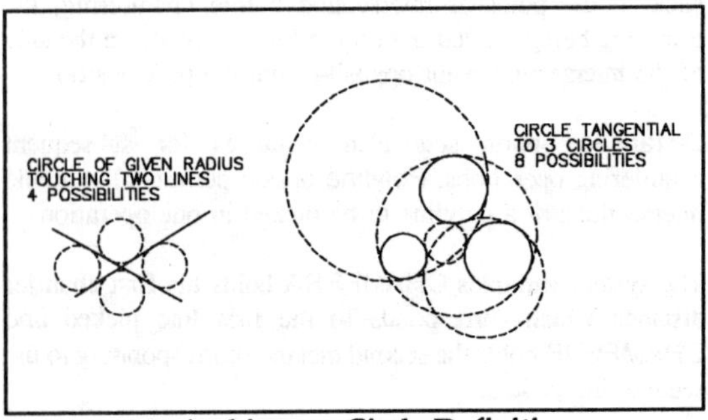

2.3 Ambiguous Circle Definitions

The system variable CIRCLERAD holds the default circle radius. The system variable VIEWRES controls the displayed resolution of circles and arcs.

DLINE
- draws double lines and arcs

Command Sequence
Command: **DLINE**
↓ **Draw → Line▸ → Double Lines**

Command Options
Double lines are useful for drawing components of constant thickness such as sheet metal fabrications. DLINE is an AutoLISP program, which explains why, when it is first used in a drafting session, a loading message is displayed. The command can be in either of two states: Line - the initial state, and Arc. Each gives a different set of options.

In Line mode, the options are:
Break/Caps/Dragline/Offset/Snap/Undo/Width/<start point>:.

After the start point has been entered, another option: /Arc appears.

In Arc mode, the options are:
Break/CAps/CEnter/CLose/Dragline/Endpoint/Line/ Snap/Undo/Width/<Second Point>:.

- Arc, after a start point has been entered, enables Arc mode to be entered.
- Line enters Line mode.
- Break results in double lines being intersected neatly.
- Caps/CAps closes double line ends and starts. The user can select from: Both/End/None/Start/<Auto>: which determine how the lines are to be closed.
- CEnter enables the centre of an arc to be defined.
- Dragline controls how the double line is disposed about pick points. The selection can be made from the list: Select position to the Left/Center/Right/<Offset from

center = default>:, Left and **Right** referring to the double line in the direction in which it is being drawn.

- **Offset** enables the specification of a double line with reference to a base point. The base point, the direction of the line and the offset distance may be defined.
- **Endpoint** completes the drawing of the double line.
- **Close** closes the double line neatly.
- **Snap** controls whether the start point or end point of a double line segment is snapped to an object. **Snap** may be turned ON or OFF and the snap distance may be defined in pixels using a size option. If **Break** is ON, the object being snapped to will be broken between the double line being joined to it.
- **Undo** removes the last double line segment defined.
- **Width** sets the separation distance of the double line segments.

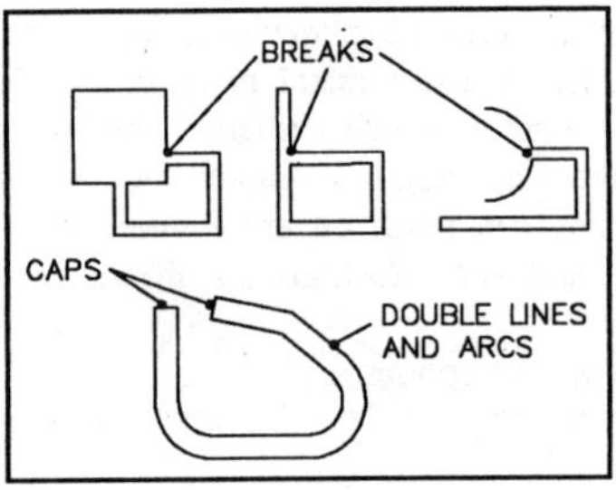

2.4 DLINE

DONUT/DOUGHNUT

- draws rings

Command Sequence

Command: **DOUGHNUT (or DONUT)**

→ **DRAW** → **DONUT:**

↓ **Draw** →**Donut**

Command Options

The inside and outside diameters of the doughnut are specified after prompts. Filled circles may be drawn by entering an inside diameter of zero. After the diameters have been specified, the centre of the doughnut must be defined. This can be repeated, further centres being defined, the procedure being terminated by entering RETURN.

Doughnuts are drawn filled if the system variable FILLMODE is ON. The system variables DONUTID and DONUTOD hold the default inside and outside diameters of doughnuts.

ELLIPSE
- draws a polyline ellipse

Command Sequence

Command: **ELLIPSE**
→ DRAW → ELLIPSE:
↓ Draw → Ellipse▸

Command Options

The ellipse can be drawn in one of two modes depending on whether rectangular coordinates or isometric coordinates are in force. The following assumes that rectangular coordinates are being used. The other case, after the command ISOPLANE has been given, is dealt with in Section 10.

An ellipse may be defined in two ways: by indicating the major and minor axes or by defining one axis and a rotational angle. Defining a rotational angle results in an ellipse which is the view of a circle rotated by that angle about a diameter in the plane of the paper. The ellipse is constructed from sixteen circular arcs, the endpoints of which are conveniently chosen.

Options of the command permit the following definitions after the prompt: <Axis endpoint 1>/Center:

- Two endpoints of an axis and the other semi-axis length.
- Two endpoints of an axis and a rotational angle.
- The ellipse centre and the two semi-axis endpoints.
- The ellipse centre, a semi-axis endpoint and a rotational angle.

FILLET
- fillets a pair of objects

Command Sequence
Command: **FILLET**
→ **EDIT** → **next** → **FILLET:**
↓ **Construct** → **Fillet**

Command Options
The prompt: Polyline/Radius/<Select first object>: is displayed. Initially, the fillet radius is set by typing R followed by the required radius. The command is then terminated and the defined radius is in force for subsequent filleting operations.

To fillet two objects, the command is repeated and the objects picked. If the combination of objects is legal (any two lines, arcs or circles), the objects will be filleted and trimmed back to the fillet.

Occasionally, there are two or more possible fillets. AutoCAD resolves the ambiguity sensibly by taking a hint from the pick positions. AutoCAD recognises fillets of zero radius. The most useful applications of this are to delete previous fillets and to extend or trim two lines to their intersection. The Polyline option permits all suitable adjacent segments of a polyline to be filleted in one operation. The system variable FILLETRAD holds the current fillet radius.

LINE
- draws single or chained straight lines

Command Sequence
Command: **LINE**
→ **DRAW** → **LINE:**
↓ **Draw** → **Line▸**

Command Options
From point: is displayed and the start of the line is defined. The endpoint of the line is defined after the prompt To point:. This prompt is repeated so that a chain of connected

lines may be drawn. A single line can be drawn by input of RETURN in response to the second To point: prompt.

If RETURN is input in response to the initial From point: prompt, the start point of the line will be assumed to be the last point defined. If the last object drawn was an arc, the line will be at the same angle as the final tangent to the arc.

Entry of U deletes the last line segment without exiting the command. This may be repeated. Entry of C draws a line from the last point defined to the first point defined, so closing the polygon.

The line font (whether full, dashed, dotted etc) may be set by the command LINETYPE. The scaling of dots and dashes is set by the command LTSCALE.

The system variable LASTPOINT holds the coordinates of the endpoint of the last line defined.

PLINE
- draws a polyline

Command Sequence
Command: **PLINE**
→ DRAW → next → PLINE:
↓ Draw → Polyline▸ → 2D

Command Options
After the initial point has been defined following the prompt From point:, the PLINE command can be in one of two states: drawing lines or drawing arcs. These states can be switched. Initially, the command enters the line state, in which the options are:

Arc/Close/Halfwidth/Length/Undo/Width/
<Endpoint of line>:

In the arc state, the options are:

Angle/CEnter/CLose/Direction/Halfwidth/Line/
Radius/Second pt/Undo/Width/<Endpoint of arc>:

In line state, arc state is entered by typing A; in arc state, line state is entered by typing L.

After the first point is defined - by entering coordinates, by picking a point or by entering RETURN to select the coordinates of the last defined point - the current linewidth is displayed. If a new linewidth is not specified, the polyline will be drawn at the current line width. The various response options may then be entered.In line state, these are:

- Close: a line of the current width is drawn from the current point to the start point and the command is terminated. This is the best way to draw closed polygons since all the segment junctions will be neatly bevelled.
- Halfwidth: prompts will be issued for half the segment start and end widths.
- Length: a line segment will be drawn at the angle of the previously drawn line segment or tangentially to the previous arc.
- Undo: the previous segment will be deleted.
- Width: prompts are returned for starting and ending widths of the lines. The line thickness is graduated from start to end width. The polyline will be drawn filled in if the system variable FILLMODE is ON.

In arc state, the options different from those in line state are:

- Angle: the subtended angle for the arc may be specified.
- CEnter: the centre point of the arc may be defined.
- CLose: the polyline is closed with an arc segment.
- Direction: the start direction of the next arc segment may be defined.
- Radius: the arc radius may be defined.
- Second pt: the second and third points of a three-point arc may be defined.

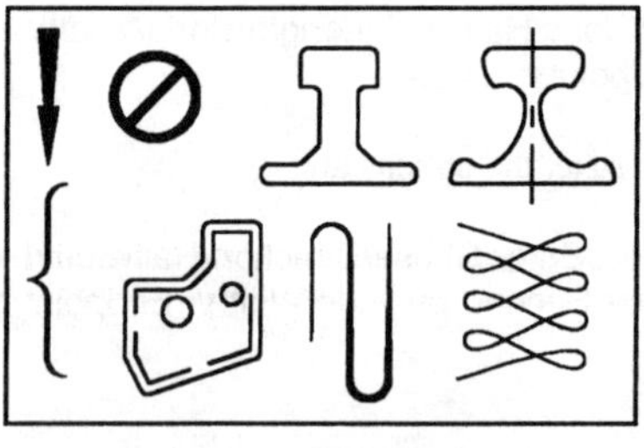

2.5 Examples of Polylines

The system variable PLINEGEN determines how linetypes are displayed at vertices. If it is set to 0, the linetype pattern starts and ends at vertices. If it is set to 1, the linetype pattern starts at the beginning of the polyline and runs continuously along it, ending at the last point.

The system variable PLINEWID holds the default polyline width.

POINT

- inserts point entities

Command Sequence

Command: **POINT**
→ **DRAW** → **next** → **POINT:**
↓ **Draw** → **Point**

Command Options

The position of the point is specified in response to the proIf the radius is supplied as a typed value, the polygon will be drawn with its bottom side horizontal. If the radius is defined by a pick and the generating circle is inscribed, thempt Point:.

The position of a point can be marked in several ways - by means of dots or crosses, for instance. The form of the mark is determined by the setting of the system variables PDMODE and PDSIZE. PDMODE holds a code which shows the form of the marker, PDSIZE holds the size of the marker - see Figure 2.7.

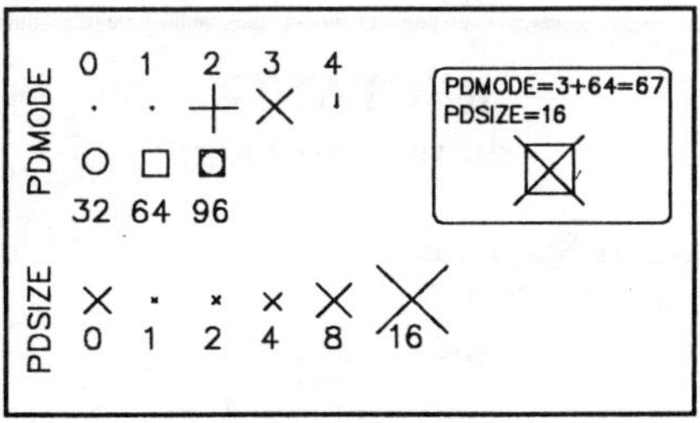

2.6 Point Markers

Points are automatically placed on a layer called DEFPOINTS when associative dimensions are drawn. The corresponding dimensions are altered if these points are re-positioned.

POLYGON
- draws a regular polygon

Command Sequence
Command: **POLYGON**
→ DRAW → next → POLYGON:
↓ Draw → Polygon

Command Options
The number of sides is provided after Number of sides.. The next prompt is: Edge/<Center of polygon>:.

If the default option is taken and the centre point of the polygon specified, the radius of a circle must be provided. There are two options for this: the radius of the inscribed circle or the radius of the circumscribed circle (the distance from the centre point to a vertex of the polygon or the distance to the midpoint of a side).

If the radius is supplied as a typed value, the polygon will be drawn with its bottom side horizontal. If the radius is defined by a pick and the generating circle is inscribed, the pick point defines a vertex of the polygon. If the radius is defined by a pick and the generating circle is circumscribed, the pick point defines the middle of a side. If the Edge option is chosen, the polygon may be drawn by supplying the endpoint of one of its sides.

RECTANG*
- draws a rectangle

Command Sequence
Command: **RECTANG**
↓ Draw → Rectangle

Command Options

Diagonally opposed corners are selected in response to prompts and the rectangle is drawn as a closed polyline.

SKETCH

-makes freehand drawings

Command Sequence

Command: **SKETCH**
→ **DRAW** → **next** → **SKETCH:**
↓ **Draw** → **Line** → **Sketch**

Command Options

SKETCH is a sub-system with its own set of commands. The sketch produced is a chain of short lines which may be edited and, if satisfactory, stored. The sketching is done by sampling the pointing device at fixed distances (or record increments). Sketching can easily use a large amount of storage, so it is important to keep the record increment size as large as possible. On the other hand, too large a record increment gives a sketch of poor quality. The balance is a matter of practice (as is the production of reasonable sketches using a mouse). After the record increment has been established in response to the prompt Record increment:, the next prompt is:

Pen eXit Quit Record Erase Connect:

- Pen: lifts and lowers the sketching device.
- eXit: leaves the SKETCH system without saving temporary lines.
- Quit: discards all unstored lines and leaves SKETCH.
- Record: saves temporary lines.
- Erase: deletes temporary lines.
- Connect: connects a raised pen to the last point input. This enables a sketch to be done in sections.

Input of a full stop draws a straight line from the end of the last sketched line to the current raised pen location. Sketching can be done in polylines instead of ordinary lines if the system variable SKPOLY is set to 1. SKETCHINC holds the current sketch increment.

2.7
SKETCH

SOLID

- draws a polygon filled or in outline

Command Sequence

Command: **SOLID**

→ **DRAW** → **next** → **SOLID:**

Command Options

Points defining the vertices of the solid are input or picked in response to prompts.The polygon is *not* built up by defining vertices successively but by defining the triangles from which it is made up. After the last vertex, typing RETURN closes the solid and exits the command.

System variable FILLMODE controls whether the solid is drawn filled or in outline. If it is set to 0, fill is disabled: if it is set to 1, fill is enabled. The command FILL may be used to set and unset FILLMODE.

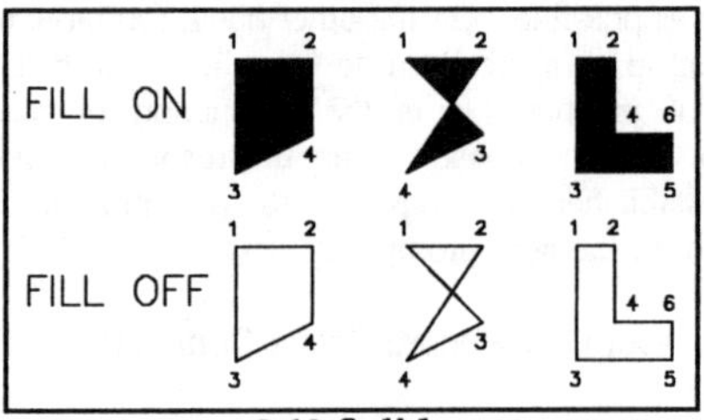

2.10 Solids

TRACE

- draws a chain of wide lines

Command Sequence

Command: **TRACE**

→ **DRAW** → **next** → **TRACE:**

Command Options

After its width has been set in response to the prompt: Trace width:, the trace is drawn by defining its line segments using start and end points. If the system variable

FILLMODE is set to 1, the trace will be drawn filled: if it is 0, the trace will be drawn in outline. FILL ON and FILL OFF may also be selected from the side menu.

The command is terminated by typing RETURN in response to a To point: prompt.

The TRACE command is a relic of early releases of AutoCAD. Although it is still available, for most purposes it is better to use the more flexible PLINE. The system variable TRACEWID holds the width of the trace.

3 Editing Commands

ALIGN*

- moves objects to align with selected points

Command Sequence

Command: **ALIGN**

↓ **Modify → Align**

Command Options

Objects are selected in response to the prompt: Select objects:. When this has been done, the prompt 1st source point: appears. A point on the selected objects is picked. The prompt 1st destination point: is displayed. A point, to which the first source point will be aligned, is picked. Either two or three pairs of points may be picked in this way. If two points are picked, the align transformation will be in 2D; if three are picked, the transformation will be in 3D (and one point must be in a different plane from the other two).

If three source and destination points were picked, the prompt: <2d> or 3d transformation: is given. The type of transformation is returned by typing either RETURN (the default) or 3.

ARRAY

- draws rectangular or circular arrays

Command Sequence

Command: **ARRAY**

→ **EDIT → ARRAY:**

↓ **Construct → Array**

Command Options

The prompt Select objects: is issued. After the objects have been selected, the type of array - rectangular (like a chessboard) or polar (like a gear wheel) must be indicated in response to the prompt Rectangular or Polar Array (R/P):.

If the Rectangular option is chosen, the command requires the number of rows, the number of columns, the distance between each row and the distance between each column. Rows run horizontally, columns (like architectural columns) stand vertically. The datum of the rectangular array is the bottom left cell. Hence, if positive distances are specified, the array extends upwards and to the right from the datum. If any other mode of extension is needed, negative distances can be used.

If the Polar option is chosen, the command requires the centre point of the array, the number of items and the angle to be subtended by the array. If these are supplied, the polar array is fully determined dimensionally.

A further piece of information must be given - whether the object is to be rotated around the centre of the array as it is drawn.

Alternatively, either the fill angle or the number of items may be left unspecified (by input of RETURN). A further prompt will be issued asking for the angle between the rotated items.

The array is set up with rows parallel with the horizontal drawing axis and columns parallel with the vertical drawing axis. If the array is to be set up at an angle relative to the current coordinates, the snap rotation angle can be adjusted using the command SNAP and subsequently drawn arrays will be aligned with it.

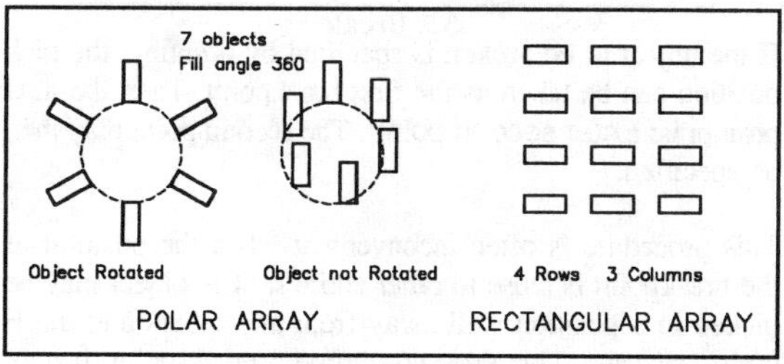

3.1 Arrays

BREAK

- removes an unwanted part of a line, arc or 2D polyline

Command Sequence

Command: **BREAK**
→ **EDIT** → **BREAK:**
↓ **Modify** → **Break▸**

Command Options

The object to be broken is specified in response to the prompt Select object:. The system then requires the specification of two points between which the object chosen is to be broken in reply to the prompts Enter first point: and Enter second point:. The portion of the entity between the two specified points is deleted. One of the points may be the endpoint of a line or arc. The ambiguity when a circle is broken is resolved by the general AutoCAD rule that the positive direction is anticlockwise.

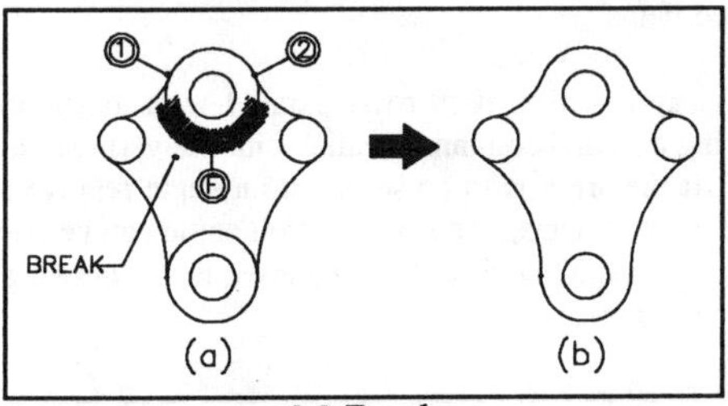

3.2 Break

If the object to be broken is specified by pointing, the pick position can be taken as the first breakpoint. Then the next prompt is: Enter second point:. The second point may then be specified.

This procedure is often inconvenient when the position of the breakpoint is close to other entities. The object may be picked in a position well away from any others and the F option chosen. This does not define a break point, it only selects the object to be broken. The two breakpoints may then be selected with no chance of ambiguity.

CHANGE

- changes the properties of existing entities

Command Sequence

Command: **CHANGE**

→ **EDIT** → **CHANGE:**

↓ **Modify** → **Change** → **Points/Properties**

Command Options

Objects selected for change by this command must have extrusion length of zero or have extrusion direction parallel with the Z-axis of the current UCS.

When the objects have been selected in response to the Select Objects: prompt, Properties/<Change point>: will be displayed and a point may be picked. This is used to modify entities in a way specific to their type. For instance:

- If the selected entity is a line, the endpoint nearer to the picked point is moved to coincide with the point.
- If the selected entity is a circle, its radius is modified so that it passes through the picked point.
- If the selected entity is text, the point becomes the new text location. Successive prompts are issued enabling text style, height, rotation angle to be altered. Also, the text itself may be edited.

If the Properties option is selected, the associated properties of the selected entities can be changed. The properties are chosen from the list given in the prompt:
Change what property(Color/Elev/LAyer/LType/ Thickness)?

When a property type is selected, the current value for the selected entity is shown and the new property to replace it is provided.

- Color. The new colour may be entered by specifying either the colour's number or its name. These are described in Display Controls. The object's colour can be made the same as that current in its layer by entering BYLAYER for the colour. If the object is to become part of a block and have the same colour as the block when it is inserted, BYBLOCK may be entered.
- Elev. The base elevation of selected entities may be set.

- Layer. The objects can be shifted from one layer to another. The name of the layer is submitted - it must have already have been created.
- LType. The linetypes associated with the selected objects may be changed. The linetype must have first been loaded - if this has not been done using the LINETYPE command, the option attempts to load it from the linetype library file. This process is described in Display Controls.
- Thickness. The object's three-dimensional thickness can be changed enabling a two-dimensional entity to be extruded in the Z-direction.

Some of the operations in CHANGE may be done instead by individual commands CHPROP and CHTEXT.

CHPROP
- changes properties of entities

Command Sequence

Command: **CHPROP**
→ **EDIT** → **CHPROP**

Command Options

Properties covered are colour, linetype, layer and thickness. CHPROP works with all entities regardless of their extrusion direction in contrast with CHANGE which only works with entities whose extrusion direction is parallel with the Z-direction of the current UCS. The Elev option is not available in CHPROP.

See CHANGE command Properties option.

COLOR
- allocates colours to objects

Command Sequence

Command: **COLOR**
→ **SETTINGS** → **COLOR:**
'COLOR (Release 12 only)

Command Options

The colour numbers and names recognised by AutoCAD are shown in Table 3.1:

NAME	NUMBER
RED	1
YELLOW	2
GREEN	3
CYAN	4
BLUE	5
MAGENTA	6
WHITE	7

Table 3.1

Numbers up to 255 may be entered; the colour displayed will depend on the graphics adaptor fitted. The selected colour is typed in either name or numeric form after the prompt New entity color <BYLAYER>:.

The keywords BYLAYER and BYBLOCK are also permitted. BYLAYER gives subsequent entities the colour allocated to the layer. BYBLOCK gives an entity used in a block the colour of the layer on which the block is placed.

COPY
- copies entities

Command Sequence

Command: **COPY**
→ **EDIT** → **COPY:**
↓ **Construct** → **Copy**

Command Options

The objects to be copied are selected after the Select Objects: prompt and a base point defined in reply to the prompt: <Base point or displacement>/Multiple:.

If just one copy is needed, then entry of another point after Second point of displacement: completes the definition of the displacement vector and the selected objects are copied.

If multiple copies are needed, the Multiple option is chosen. A base point is entered followed by a succession of second points. Each of these results in a copy with the original basepoint placed at the second points. RETURN terminates the command. If DRAG is entered instead of a base point, the objects can be dragged visually into position.

DDCHPROP*

- changes properties of entities

Command Sequence

Command: **DDCHPROP**

↓ **Modify → Change → Properties**

Command Options

DDCHPROP acts like CHPROP except that changes are selected through dialogue boxes. After objects have been selected, the Change Properties dialogue box appears. This box has one edit box in which a new entity thickness may be typed. It also has three buttons corresponding to changes of colour, layer and linetype. Each of these has its own dialogue box which appears if the button is clicked.

- The Select Colour box contains palettes: the standard colours, shades of gray and full colour from which a colour can be chosen. Colours may also be chosen BYLAYER and BYBLOCK.

- The Select Linetype box has a list showing all the linetypes currently loaded. A linetype may be chosen from the list or its name may be typed in directly.

- The Select Layer box has a list of names of all layers defined in the drawing. A layer may be chosen from the list or its name typed in directly.

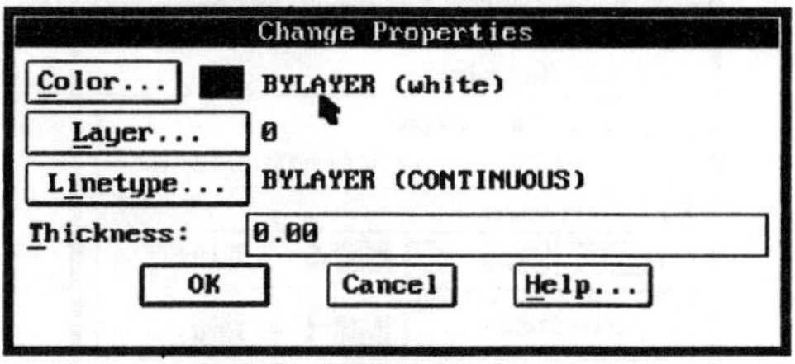

3.3 DDCHPROP Dialogue Box

DDGRIPS*

- controls grip display

Command Sequence

Command: **DDGRIPS**

↓ **Settings** → **Grips...**

'DDGRIPS

Command Options

One of the most apparent differences between Release 12 and earlier versions is the provision of grips. Grips are marks which are placed at characteristic positions on entities. They can be used to edit entities very quickly and conveniently. The crosshair cursor may be snapped to a grip. This is shown by the grip changing colour - or becoming a "hot grip". One of a series of edits may be performed on the entity, cycling through the options available by entering RETURN or pressing the right button on the mouse, possibly repeatedly. Editing operations possible in this way are STRETCH, MOVE, ROTATE, SCALE and MIRROR.

DDGRIPS enables and disables grips. A dialogue box is displayed containing two check boxes used to enable or disable grips on primitive entities and within blocks. There is also provision for changing the initial colour of grips, for defining the colour when the grip becomes "hot" and for adjusting the size of the grip square.

Grips may also be enabled and disabled by setting or unsetting the system variable GRIPS.

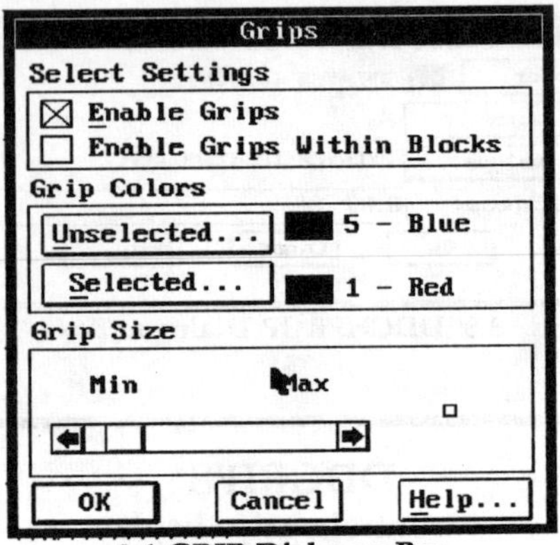

3.4 GRIP Dialogue Box

DDMODIFY

- changes the characteristics of entities

Command Sequence

Command: **DDMODIFY**

→ EDIT → DDMODFY:

↓ Modify → Entity...

Command Options

The procedure after an entity has been picked depends on the type of entity. A dialogue box is displayed, its form being specialised to the entity type. Figure 3.5 shows the dialogue box displayed if a circle has been selected. Properties such as the centre, radius, and linetype may be modified using the buttons and edit windows of the dialogue box.

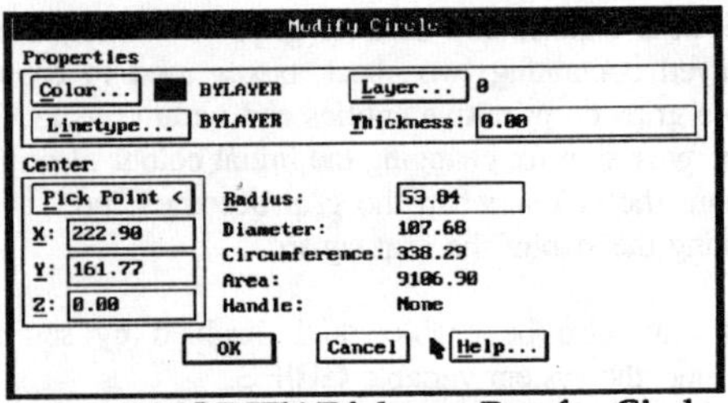

3.5 DDMODIFY Dialogue Box for Circle

Buttons on this box, when hit, result in the display of other, specialised boxes. Entities and properties which can be modified are:

- Arcs; radius, centre, start and end angles
- Attribute definitions: origin point, height, width, rotation angle etc
- Blocks: insertion point, scale factors, rotaton angle etc
- Circles: centre, radius
- Points: position
- Polylines: vertex positions, linetype etc
- Shapes: origin, size, rotation angle etc
- Solids and traces: vertex positions
- Text: message, style, justification etc
- 3DFaces: vertex locations, edge visibility.

DDSELECT*
- forms a selection for use in editing and other commands

Command Sequence
Command: **DDSELECT**
↓ Settings → Selection Settings...

Command Options
The Entity Selection Settings dialogue box is displayed - see Figure 3.6.

3.6 DDSELECT Dialogue Box

The dialogue box contains four check boxes which govern how objects are selected.

- Noun/Verb Selection. This inverts the normal AutoCAD command structure. An object can be picked and a command issued detailing how it is to be edited.
- Use Shift to Add. This enables more than one object to be picked in the same operation. One object is picked, then additional objects picked when the SHIFT key is down.
- Press and Drag. Normally, a window or crossing box needs two picks, one at each of two diagonally opposite corners. With Press and Drag, one pick is made and the other obtained by dragging the mouse with the button still depressed.
- Implied Windowing. Without this option in force, a window is obtained by first typing W, a crossing box by first typing C. With Implied Windowing, a window can be obtained by clicking on a corner, then dragging to the other corner in a left to right direction. A crossing box can be obtained by dragging in a right to left direction.

There is, below these check boxes, a button labelled Default Selection Mode which may be used to reset selection modes to default conditions. There is a scroll bar used to change the size of the pick aperture. This can be varied from one to 20 pixels. A further button, titled Entity Sort Method, calls up a secondary dialogue box that may be used to change the method of arranging entities in the AutoCAD database. Before Release 12, entities were sorted in the order in which they were created, which sometimes led to difficulties of selecting entities close together. Entities can now be sorted in various ways specialised to different applications: Object Selection, Object Snap, Redraws, Slide Creation, Regenerations, Plotting, and Postscript Output.

DIVIDE

- places equi-spaced markers along an entity

Command Sequence

Command: **DIVIDE**
→ **EDIT** → **DIVIDE:**
↓ **Construct** → **Divide**

Command Options

The object picked must be a line, an arc, a circle or a polyline. It is selected after the prompt: Select object to divide:. The next prompt is: <Number of segments>/Block:. If a number between 2 and 32767 is entered, the picked entity will be divided into that number of parts, point entities being placed at each point of division.

If the Block option is chosen, the marker will be a block (which must be currently defined in the drawing). In this case, the prompts will be:

Block name to insert:
Align block with object? <Y>:
Number of segments:

The block may placed either in its stored alignment or rotated at each position so that it aligns with the divided object. On a polyline, the division starts at the first node defined. On a circle, the first division starts at a point which is located at the current snap rotation angle from the centre. Notice that the division only involves the placing of markers for construction purposes - the object is unchanged.

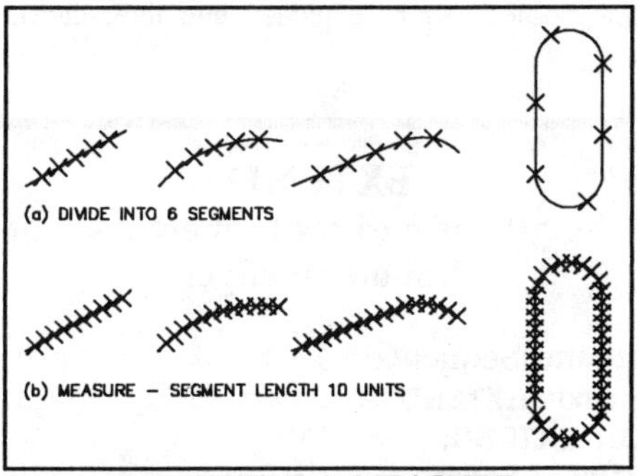

3.7 DIVIDE & MEASURE

ERASE

- removes unwanted entities

Command Sequence

Command: **ERASE**
→ **EDIT** → **ERASE:**
↓ **Modify** → **Erase▸**

Command Options

Objects are selected in response to the prompt Select objects:. They will then be erased. If it is wished to reinstate them, the command OOPS can be used.

EXPLODE

- dismembers a composite entity into its component parts

Command Sequence

Command: **EXPLODE**
→ **EDIT** → **EXPLODE:**
↓ **Modify** → **Explode**

Command Options

Select block reference, polyline, dimension or mesh: is displayed and an object selected. The selected object will then be exploded. Polylines will be exploded into line and arc segments; their widths will be lost. Inserted blocks will be exploded into the entities of which they are composed. Polygon meshes will be exploded into three-dimensional faces.

EXTEND

- lengthens entities to meet a set of boundary edges

Command Sequence

Command: **EXTEND**
→ **EDIT EXTEND:**
↓ **Modify** → **Extend**

Command Options

A set of objects, to which the selected objects are to be extended, are picked in response to the prompt Select boundary edge(s)... These boundary edges must lie in the extended length of the objects to be extended. The objects to be extended are selected after a second prompt: <Select objects to extend>/Undo:. The point picked on the object is used as a clue to the direction of extension.

Neither the edges nor the objects to be extended can be blocks and the objects to be extended must lie in a plane parallel with the current user coordinate system. The Undo option is unavailable prior to Release 11.

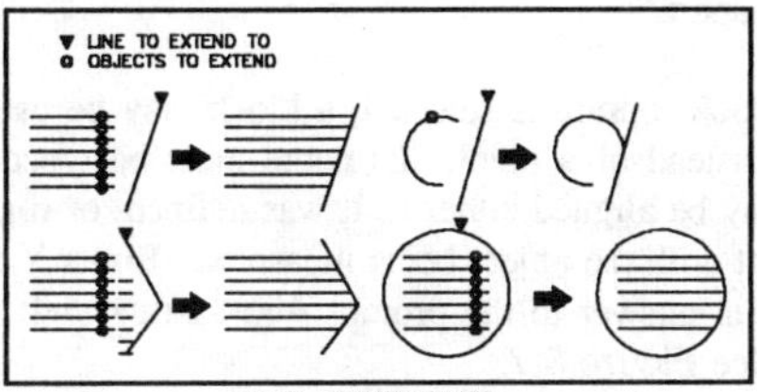

3.8 EXTEND

FILL

- enables and disables the solid fill of polylines, solids and traces

Command Sequence

Command: **FILL**
'FILL (Release 12 only)

Command Options

The prompt for the FILL command is ON/OFF: When FILL is ON, polylines, solids and traces are filled in. When FILL is OFF, only their outlines will be shown. This is mainly used to save regeneration time.

FILL sets or unsets the system variable FILLMODE; this may also be done using the SETVAR command.

MEASURE

- places markers at a specified distance apart along an entity

Command Sequence

Command: **MEASURE:**
→ **EDIT** → **next** → **MEASURE:**
↓ **Construct** → **Measure**

Command Options

Select object to measure: is displayed. One object is selected for measuring. A second prompt is issued: <Segment length>/Block:. A distance is provided and marker points are placed along the object's length that distance apart.

If the Block: option is selected, a block may be used as a marker instead of a point. Its name must be typed. The block may be aligned either as it was defined, or rotated to alignment with the object being measured. Either Y or N is returned in answer to the prompt Align block with object <Y>:. See Figure 3.7.

MIRROR

- draws a mirror-image of a set of objects

Command Sequence

Command: **MIRROR**

→ **EDIT** → **next** → **MIRROR**

↓ **Construct** → **Mirror**

Command Options

The objects to be mirrored are selected after the Select objects: prompt, then two points are defined on the line about which the objects are to be mirrored, the prompts being First point of mirror line: and Second point:. The original objects may be left in position by answering N or RETURN to Delete old objects? <N>:. Text will be mirrored also unless the system variable MIRRTEXT is set to 0.

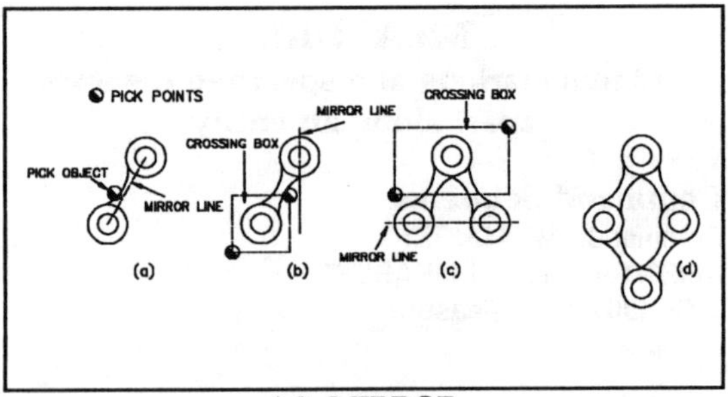

3.9 MIRROR

MOVE

- moves entities from one position to another

Command Sequence

Command: **MOVE**
→ **EDIT** → **next** → **MOVE:**
↓ **Modify** → **Move**

Command Options

When a selection of objects has been made after the prompt Select objects:, a displacement vector must be entered, the defining points being picked after the prompts: Base point or displacement: and Second point of displacement:.

The set of selected objects will be moved the distance between the reference points and at the angle between the line joining the points and the X-axis. This is the most common way of specifying the displacement vector: picking a convenient reference point on the objects and then picking the point to which the reference point is to move. However, if RETURN is entered at the prompt for the second point, the first point is interpreted as a distance vector relative to the current origin.

If DRAG is entered at the first prompt, the selected objects can be dragged into position visually.

OFFSET

- draws a parallel entity of the same type as a specified entity at a given distance from it

Command Sequence

Command: **OFFSET**
→ **DRAW** → **OFFSET:**
→ **EDIT** → **next** → **OFFSET:**
↓ **Construct** → **Offset**

Command Options

The first prompt is: Offset distance or Through<last>:. A distance may be typed in and the side of the object on which the offset is to be drawn indicated by picking a point on that side after Side to offset?. The offset distance is retained as default so that several complex forms may be given the same offset in separate operations. Another method of offsetting is to select the Through option and define the position of the offset by specifying a point through which it is to pass.

The object to be offset is picked after the next prompt: Select object to offset:. Lines, arcs, circles and two-dimensional polylines may be offset.

An offset may be drawn to a polyline in one operation although, if the polyline is complicated, the result may not be quite what was intended.

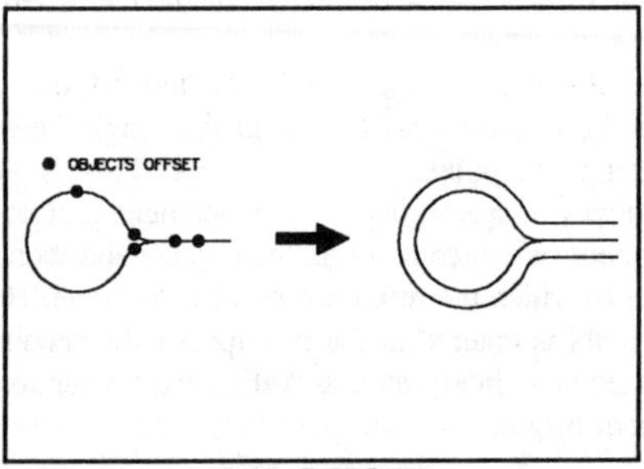

3.10 OFFSET

The offset distance is stored in the system variable OFFSETDIST which may be set outside this command.

OOPS
- restores erased objects

Command Sequence

Command: **OOPS**
→ **BLOCKS** → **BLOCK:** → **OOPS**
→ **EDIT** → **ERASE:** → **OOPS:**
↓ **Modify** → **Erase** → **Oops!**

Command Options

OOPS acts like the command U, but is specialised to restoring entities removed by the last ERASE, BLOCK or WBLOCK command.

PEDIT
- edits polylines

Command Sequence
Command: **PEDIT**
→ **EDIT** → **next** → **PEDIT:**
↓ **Modify** → **PolyEdit**

Command Options
The command can be used to edit three-dimensional polylines and meshes; only the two dimensional options will be dealt with here.

An entity is selected after Select polyline:. If it is not a polyline but a simple line or arc, the option returned is: Entity selected is not a polyline Do you want to turn it into one? <Y>:. If the answer is N, the command is terminated. If the answer is Y, the entity will be converted into a polyline and the command proceeds.

If the object was a two-dimensional polyline or has just been turned into one, a set of options will be displayed:
Close/Join/Width/Edit vertex/Fit/Spline/Decurve/
Ltypegen/Undo/eXit <X>:.

If the object was a three-dimensional polyline or mesh, another set of options will be displayed. For the three-dimensional options, see Working in 3D. The 2D options are:

- Close: Draws a segment which connects the current vertex of the polyline to the first vertex creating a closed figure.
- Open: Reverses Close. If this option is selected, the option toggles to Close (and *vice-versa*).
- Join: Allows separate segments to be joined into one polyline. The segments must have the potential to become a polyline - they must be connected exactly.
- Width: Allocates a constant width to all segments.
- Edit vertex: A vertex of the polyline is selected and various editing actions performed on it. A marker is set on the selected vertex and this can be moved along the polyline from vertex to vertex.
    - Next/Previous: moves the marker to an adjoining vertex, either forward or backwards.

- Break: breaks the polyline at the current vertex.
- Insert: adds a new node after the current vertex.
- Move: allows the current vertex to be relocated.
- Regen: regenerates the polyline - draws it with all the changes shown.
- Straighten: draws a straight line segment between the current and the next selected vertices.
- Tangent: adds a tangent direction to the current vertex. This is used in the Fit curve option in the main PEDIT command.
- Width: allows a change of start and end widths in the segment after the current vertex.
- eXit: returns from the Edit vertex subsystem to the main PEDIT command.

- Fit curve: converts a polyline composed of straight line segments into a smooth curve which is fitted taking account of any tangent information added in the Edit Vertex option. The curve is made up from arcs.
- Spline curve: uses lines joining vertices of the polyline as the control lines of a spline curve. Quadratic or cubic B-spline curves can be selected. The type of spline is governed by the setting of the SPLINETYPE system variable: quadratic = 5; cubic = 6. The control lines of a spline curve will be displayed if the system variable SPLFRAME is set to 1. The SPLINESEGS system variable controls the number of line segments used to draw the spline, a higher number giving a smoother curve.
- Ltype gen: enables lines to be drawn with linetype pattern continuous from start to end of polyline.
- Decurve: joins all the original vertices of the polyline by straight segments. Any vertices added by the curve fitting options are deleted.
- Undo: undoes the last PEDIT operation.
- eXit: leaves PEDIT.

REDO

- restores a command undone with U or UNDO

Command Sequence

Command: **REDO**
→ * * * * → **REDO:**
↓ **Assist** → **Redo**

Command Options

One UNDO or U command can be redone using this command.

ROTATE

- rotates entities about a point

Command Sequence

Command: **ROTATE**

→ **EDIT** → **next** → **ROTATE:**

↓ **Modify** → **Rotate**

Command Options

The Select objects: prompt is displayed and the objects for rotation are selected. A base point must then be defined after Base point:. This is the point in the current construction plane about which rotation will be performed.

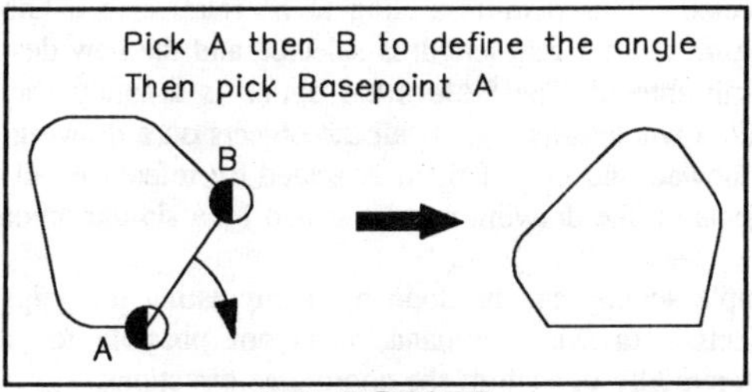

3.11 ROTATE

The rotation angle is specified after the prompt: <Rotation angle>/Reference:. An angle, obeying the AutoCAD convention of a positive angle being anticlockwise, may be typed explicitly. Or, the Reference option may be chosen. In this case, the rotation angle is defined by specifying a current angle and the angle which it is to become after rotation. The objects selected are then rotated by the difference between the angles.

Angles may be typed directly or may be defined by picking two points. This option is most useful when an object is to be rotated so that it aligns with another object.

SCALE

- scales entities about a reference point

Command Sequence

Command: **SCALE**

EDIT → next → SCALE:

↓ Modify → Scale

Command Options

The prompt Select objects: is issued: and the objects which are to be scaled are selected. Scaling is done around a reference point picked after Base point:. The selected objects are to be scaled about the base point, the position of which will remain unchanged.

When objects have been selected and the base point defined, the next prompt is: <Scale factor>/Reference:. A scale factor may be explicitly supplied or the Reference option selected. This permits scaling to be relative to a known length. An existing length is selected and the new desired length entered. The Reference option is a handy way to scale a whole drawing. If all the objects on a drawing are windowed and one of them is scaled by reference, all the objects on the drawing will be scaled by a similar amount.

Simple scaling can be done by manipulating the grips of objects. In this command, it is not possible to scale differentially in each of the coordinate directions.

SELECT

- defines a set of objects for subsequent operations

Command Sequence

Command: **SELECT**

EDIT → next → SELECT:

Command Options

At each selection, the normal screen crosshairs are replaced by an object selection box, which is used to select objects without having to be exact. The size of the box is governed by the value of the system variable PICKBOX. This contains the height of the box in pixels and can be set to suit personal preference using the SETVAR command or by typing PICKBOX directly.

Selection may be done in various ways, each having an option abbreviation. Each candidate for selection is highlighted on the screen.

- Point: searches the drawing file for an entity passing through a point either picked or referenced by typing coordinates.
- Multiple: delays the search for selected objects until several picks have been made. The scan is carried out when RETURN is returned to the prompt. This option can speed up object selection considerably if many entities are to be selected from a large drawing file.
- Window: defines a rectangular window by picking two diagonally opposite corners. Any entity lying wholly within the window is selected.
- Crossing: is similar to the Window option except that entities need not be wholly within the window in order to be selected.
- Box: is the same as Windows, if diagonal corners are selected in left to right order. If the order is right to left, Box is the same as Crossing.
- AUto: selects an entity found in the Object Selection box. If none is found, then the pick point is assumed to be the first definition point of a Box.
- Last: selects the last entity created.
- Previous: restores the most recent selection set.
- Undo: removes the most recently added group of entities from the current selection set.
- Remove: changes the command mode so that objects picked are deleted from the selection set.
- Add: changes the command mode so that objects picked are added to the selection set. This is the default mode.
- SIngle: disables the repeat of the Select objects: prompt.

The following options are only available in Release 12:

- ALL: selects all the entities in the drawing.
- CPolygon: selects all entities in or crossing an irregular polygon defined by picking its vertices.
- Fence: selects all entities crossed by a Fence line which is defined by picking its endpoints.
- WPolygon: selects all entities enclosed within an

irregular polygon defined by picking its endpoints.

RETURN terminates selection and leaves the command. CTRL-C exits the command and clears the selection set. At each selection, the command shows a count of the objects selected currently and the number found at the last selection operation. All the options are available in the Select object: prompt which occurs in most of the editing commands.

STRETCH

- moves vertices of objects preserving connectivity

Command Sequence

Command: **STRETCH**
→ **EDIT** → **next** → **STRETCH:**
↓ **Modify** → **Stretch**

Command Options

The first prompt issued is: Select objects to stretch by window... Select objects:. The objects to be stretched are selected by using a Crossing window. Objects which are not to be stretched but have been selected may be removed by using the Remove option. When this has been done, the command continues: Base point: and then New point:

The base-point is selected and the new point is rubber-banded to it. The selected objects will be stretched. This operation does not work on text or blocks, which will be moved bodily and unchanged in form.

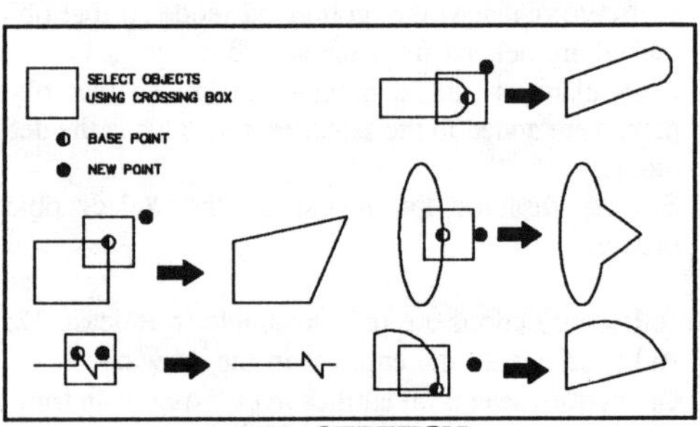

3.12 STRETCH

TRIM

- trims back entities to meet other entities

Command Sequence.

Command: **TRIM**
→ **EDIT** → **next** → **TRIM:**
↓ **Modify** → **Trim**

Command Options

Objects, which act as trim boundaries, are selected successively in answer to the prompt: Select cutting edge(s)... When this has been completed (by entering RETURN), the objects for trimming must be picked. <Select objects to trim>/Undo: is displayed.

For successful trimming, the cutting edges must intersect the objects to be trimmed. Neither the cutting edges nor the objects for trimming can be blocks. If two cutting edges cut an entity to be trimmed, the segment between the edges will be trimmed. As is usual in AutoCAD, ambiguity is resolved sensibly by taking a hint from the position of the picked points

The UNDO option returns selected objects to the untrimmed state.

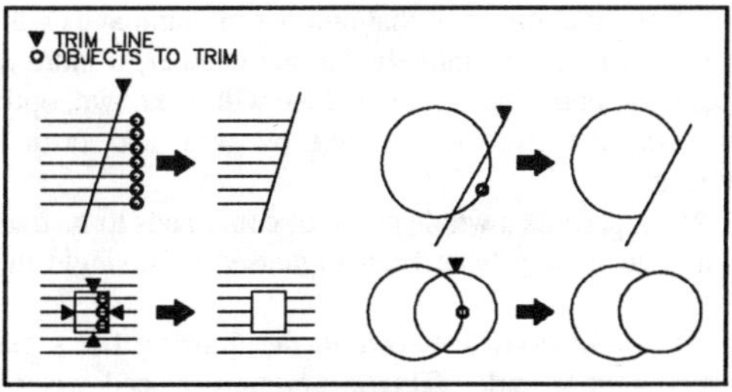

3.13 TRIM

U

- removes the effects of the most recent command

Command Sequence

Command: **U**

→ *** * * *** → **U:**

↓ **Assist** → **UNDO**

Command Options

This command is used to reverse just one command but may be repeated if necessary right back to the beginning of the session. Some commands by their nature cannot be undone, for instance PLOT.

UNDO

- reverses several commands

Command Sequence

Command: **UNDO**

→ **EDIT** → **next** → **UNDO:**

Command Options

Auto/Back/Control/End/Group/Mark/<default number>: is displayed. If the default option is taken, a number is entered and the effects of that number of commands will be reversed. Since it is unlikely that the number, if more than a couple, of commands to be undone will be known, options permitting the user to proceed by trial and error are provided.

- Auto: permits a whole group of commands to be treated as one if they have been organised as a single menu item.
- Mark: positions a marker in the drawing file - rather like a bookmark. This is normally placed when the current state of the drawing is satisfactory and some speculative operations are to be done. The drawing may be then be worked on and, if the desired result be not achieved, the drawing file may be undone back to the last mark by using the Back option.
- Back: undoes all commands back to the position where the drawing file was marked.

- **Group** and **End**: work as parentheses so that a group of commands can be treated as one. A block of commands bracketed with **Group** and **End** may be undone in one operation using the **U** command.
- **Control**: modifies the action of the UNDO command. Available options may be adjusted by:
  - **All** fully enables the UNDO command.
  - **None** full disables the UNDO command.
  - **One** restricts UNDO to just one command.

4 Display Controls

APERTURE

- adjusts size of object snap target box

Command Sequence
Command: **APERTURE**
→ **SETTINGS** → **APERTUR:**

Command Options
The OSNAP target box can be sized to suit user preference. Too large a box is undesirable because it is difficult to select an object from a densely populated part of the drawing. Too small a box is undesirable because the precision needed to select an object slows up working. The size is set in response to the prompt: Object snap target height (1-50 pixels) <current size>:. The aperture size is held in the system variable APERTURE.

BLIPMODE

- controls display of blips

Command Sequence
Command: **BLIPMODE**
→ **SETTINGS** → **BLIPS:**

Command Options
Blips are small marks displayed at picked points. They can be turned on or off using this command. The command sets a system variable BLIPMODE.

DDUCS

- sets the user coordinate system

Command Sequence
Command: **DDUCS**
→ **UCS:** → **DDUCS:**
↓ **Settings** → **UCS▸** → **Named UCS...**
↓ **Settings** → **UCS▸** → **Preset...**

Command Options

The UCS Control dialogue box is displayed. Dialogue box options are:

- Current: selects current UCS.
- UCS Name: displays names of UCS's currently defined. Enables UCS names to be changed.
- List: displays information about UCS's.
- Delete: deletes a UCS.
- OK: stores UCS settings held in the dialogue box and exits.
- Cancel: exits the dialogue box ignoring its settings.

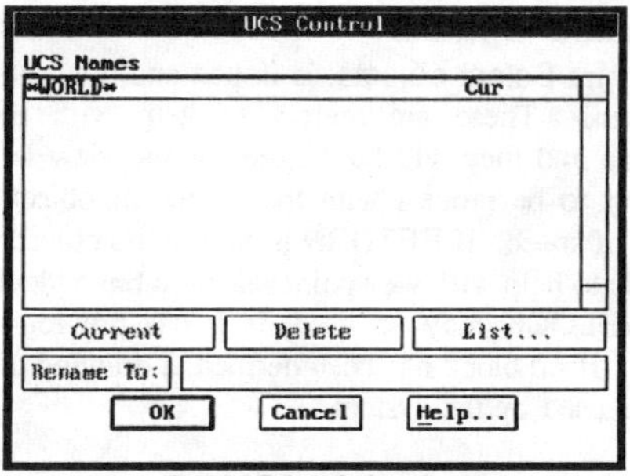

4.1 DDUCS Dialogue Box

System variables influenced by this command are detailed under the UCS command described in this section. The appearance of UCS icons is shown in Section 1.

DRAGMODE
- enables or disables object drag

Command Sequence

Command: **DRAGMODE**
→ **SETTINGS** → **DRAGMOD:**

Command Options

The prompt: ON/OFF/Auto: is issued.

- ON: enables the drag facility.
- OFF: disables the drag facility.
- Auto: allows all operations that naturally support dragging to do so regardless of the setting.

This command sets the system variable DRAGMODE. ON =1, OFF = 0, AUTO = 2.

DVIEW

- sets up views of 3D models

Command Sequence

Command: **DVIEW**

→ **DISPLAY** → **DVIEW:**

↓ **View** → **Set View▸** → **Dview**

Command Options

The prompt Select objects: is issued and a set of objects is chosen. These are merely to help with the view definition and they will be dragged as the view is altered. It is best to be modest with the choice of objects in the interest of speed. If RETURN is chosen, no objects will be available to help with viewpoint selection but a block called DVIEWBLOCK may be used, if it has previously been defined. If no block has been defined, a drawing of a little house is used by the system.

The major prompt is now displayed. This is:
CAmera/TArget/Distance/POints/PAn/Zoom/TWist/CLip/Hide/Off/Undo/<eXit>:

CAmera: permits the the viewpoint to be moved around as if a camera were being aimed. The option requires two angles as parameter; the angle on the XY plane and the angle from the XY plane. These define the horizontal and vertical view angles relative to the target. They may be entered either explicitly or by using a pair of slide bars, one for each angle.

TArget: allows the camera to be pointed in different directions while keeping its location constant. Again, these directions are either typed in or defined using a pair of slide bars.

Distance: turns on perspective mode. Parallel projections appear the same from any distance, so if that type of projection is required, the Distance option is not taken. The distance between the camera and the target is typed in or defined using a slider bar at the top of the screen.

POints: allows the camera position and target location to be entered directly.

PAn: moves both camera position and target point together relative to the current UCS. As with the normal PAN command, which cannot be used in the perspective mode, a basepoint and point of displacement are required.

Zoom: zooms the image in and out. If parallel projection is in force, a zoom factor must be entered. If viewing is in perspective mode, a lens focal length is required. Both may be done by typing a value or by using a slider bar. The normal ZOOM command cannot be used in perspective mode.

TWist: rotates the view about the line of sight. An angle of rotation must be defined.

CLip: hides unwanted parts of the view such as foreground objects which obscure other objects which are needed in the image. Two clipping planes may be set up, one in front of the desired image, one behind. The distances from the target to these planes is defined in response to Back/Front/<Off>:. Again, a slider bar may be used to set up the planes dynamically.

Hide: removes hidden lines from the objects selected for display.

Off: switches from perspective mode to parallel projection.

Undo: is used to undo previous DVIEW operations one by one.

eXit: leaves DVIEW and regenerates the drawing. The operations carried out in DVIEW are now carried out on all objects in the drawing, not just the ones selected to aid dynamic viewing.

The system variables connected with DVIEW are: BACKZ, FRONTZ, TARGET, VIEWCTR, VIEWDIR, VIEWMODE, VIEWSIZE, VIEWTWIST and WORLDVIEW.

GRAPHSCR

- flips the display to graphics mode

Command Sequence

Command: **GRAPHSCR**
'GRAPHSCR
F1

Command Options

This command is used in conjunction with TEXTSCR to flip the screen between graphics mode - the normal drawing screen - and text mode - used for display of text.

The command is not normally useful in ordinary drafting. It is used, for instance, inside AutoLISP programs. Some installations have two screens, one for text display and one for graphics. On a single display system, the function key F1 is normally used to toggle between text and graphics displays.

MENU

- loads custom menus

Command Sequence

Command: **MENU**
→ UTILITY → MENU:

Command Options

If the system variable FILEDIA is set to 0, the prompt Menu file name or . for none <acad>: appears. The required menu file name is input. If the FILEDIA is 1, meaning that a dialogue box should be displayed whenever possible, the Select Menu File dialogue box is displayed. A menu name may be selected form the list displayed.

AutoCAD provides a facility for users to design their own specialised menus. These are stored in files; source files with extension MNU, compiled files with extension MNX. The MENU command loads a menu file. The standard AutoCAD menu file is ACAD.MNU. This is the default name. If no menu is to be displayed, a period should be entered at the prompt. Otherwise, the customised menu name should be entered. An extension is unnecessary.

The system variable MENUNAME (read only) holds the name of the current menu file. MENUECHO controls how the menu works. MENUCTL controls whether the side menu changes when a command is entered from the keyboard.

MSPACE

- switches from Paperspace to Modelspace

Command Sequence

Command: **MSPACE**
→ **MVIEW** → **MSPACE**
↓ **View** → **Model Space**

Command Options

For MSPACE to work, the drawing editor must already be in Paperspace. At least one viewport must have been created in Paperspace and the system variable TILEMODE must not be 0.

The current type of space - Paperspace or Modelspace - is easily detected by the form of the UCS icon. See Section 1- Using AutoCAD for further details.

MVIEW

- creates viewports in Paperspace

Command Sequence

Command: **MVIEW**
→ **MVIEW**
→ **DISPLAY**→ **MVIEW:**
↓ **View** → **Mview▸**

Command Options

The prompt ON/OFF/Hideplot/Fit/2/3/4/Restore/<First point>: is displayed. The default option expects a point to be defined. This is taken as one corner of the Paperspace viewport. Another point is taken as the diagonally opposed corner and the viewport is set up. Other options are:

- ON/OFF: turns on or off the display of Modelspace in the selected viewport.
- Hideplot: controls removal of hidden lines for viewports when they are being plotted.
- 2/3/4: creates 2, 3 or 4 viewports. When one of these numbers is typed, the viewports can be defined by picking points. Alternatively, the viewports can be fitted automatically into the drawing area. For 2 viewports, the screen may be halved horizontally or vertically. For 3 viewports, the screen may be divided into three horizontally or vertically. Or one large and two smaller viewports may be created. For 4 viewports, the screen is divided into four viewports.
- Restore: converts viewports created using the VPORT command (which are Modelspace viewports) into Paperspace viewports. After this option is selected and the name of the window configuration has been entered, the prompt Fit/<First point>: appears. Fit scales the restored viewports to fit the drawing area. If the default option is selected, two points are picked to define the corners of the area in which the restored viewport is to be displayed.

The system variable TILEMODE must be set to 1 for this command to work.

PAN

- moves the drawing across the display

Command Sequence

Command: **PAN**
→ **DISPLAY** → **PAN:**
↓ **View** → **Pan**
'PAN (if no regeneration is needed)

Command Options

A point on the drawing is picked in response to the prompt: Displacement:. This is a reference point. The point to which this point is to move after the pan is picked after: Second point:.

PLAN

- sets a plan view in a UCS or the WCS

Command Sequence

Command: **PLAN**
→ **DISPLAY** → **PLAN:**
↓ **View** → **Set View▸** → **Plan View▸**

Command Options

The prompt is <Current UCS>/UCS/World:. If the default option is chosen, a plan view of the current UCS (or User Coordinate System) results. If UCS is chosen, a prompt asking for the name of a saved UCS is given. A list of currently defined UCS's may be obtained before the name is entered. The World option results in the display of a plan view in the World Coordinate System. The term "plan view" means a view normal to the X-Y plane in the view. The system variable UCSNAME holds the name of the current UCS.

PSPACE

- switches drawing space from Modelspace to Paperspace

Command Sequence

Command: **PSPACE**
→ **MVIEW** → **PSPACE:**
↓ **View** → **Paper Space**

Command Options

If the system variable TILEMODE is set to 0, a switch is made to Paperspace. If TILEMODE is set to 1, an error message results. In Paperspace, the UCS icon will change to a triangle (Scc Section 1).

Paperspace is an alternative working area on which views of the model can be arranged. Once in Paperspace, MVIEW may be used to set up multiple viewports which can display different views of the Modelspace drawing.

REDRAW/REDRAWALL
- refreshes the display

Command Sequence
Command: **REDRAW/REDRAWALL**
→ **DISPLAY** → **REDRAW:/REDRAWALL**
→ *** * * *** → **REDRAW:/REDRAWALL:**
↓ **View** → **Redraw/Redraw All**
'REDRAW/'REDRAWALL

Command Options
Often, during drawing sessions, parts of a drawing are removed during editing. Also, if BLIPMODE = 1, each pick results in a blip being shown. The drawing can be cleaned up using REDRAW. This only acts on the currently active viewport. REDRAWALL has a similar action except that it acts on all active viewports.

REGEN/REGENALL
- regenerates the display to show changes in drawing database

Command Sequence
Command: **REGEN/REGENALL**
→ **DISPLAY** → **REGEN:/REGNALL:**

Command Options
A regeneration causes all the drawing database to be read and all the locations of the drawn objects recalculated. REGEN also tries to optimise the number of small straight lines which make up arcs and circles.

REGEN only regenerates the current viewport. REGENALL regenerates the views in all active viewports.

REGENAUTO

- turns automatic screen regeneration on and off

Command Sequence

Command: **REGENAUTO**
→ **DISPLAY** → **RGNAUTO:**
'REGENAUTO (Release 12 only)

Command Options

Certain AutoCAD commands may result in regeneration. BLOCK, LAYER, LTSCALE and ZOOM are examples. REGENAUTO can be used to make the regenerations automatic. The prompt ON/OFF: is issued. If OFF is selected, subsequent commands requiring regeneration will prompt: About to regen, proceed? <Y>:. N aborts the command. If ON is selected, regeneration will be performed automatically.

Since regeneration of a large drawing can take a long time, it is advisable not to use REGENAUTO indiscriminately. The system variable REGENMODE is 1 if regeneration is automatic, 0 otherwise. The system variable EXPERT may be set to 1 to suppress the About to Regen, proceed? message.

TEXTSCR

- flips the display to the text screen

Command Sequence

Command: **TEXTSCR**
'TEXTSCR
F1

Command Options

If a single video display is being used, it may be in one of two modes - graphic, when it is displaying pictures and text, when it is displaying messages. If the system is in graphics mode, it can be changed to text mode by using this command. If a dual monitor system is being used, the command is ignored. In practice, the command, like GRAPHSCR, is not used while in the drawing editor because using the function toggle key F1 is more convenient. TEXTSCR and GRAPHSCR are used in applications such as script files.

UCS
- defines a new coordinate system

Command Sequence
Command: **UCS**
→ **UCS:**
↓ **Settings** → **UCS▸**

Command Options
The drawing is set in a system of coordinates called the World Coordinate System (WCS). This is often inconvenient when working in three dimensions. A local set of coordinates can be set up using the UCS command. DDUCS, the dialogue box equivalent, may also be used.

Origin/Zaxis/3point/Entity/View/X/Y/Z/Prev/Restore/Save/Del/?/<World>: is displayed.

- Origin: defines a new UCS by specification of an origin relative to the current UCS. The X, Y and Z axes are parallel to those of the old UCS. If the coordinates are preceded by an asterisk, they will be interpreted as being relative to the WCS.
- Zaxis: requires an origin point and a point along the Z-axis of the new UCS.
- 3point: defines the new UCS by three points: the origin, a point along the positive direction of the X-axis and a point along the positive direction of the Y-axis.
- Entity: defines the new UCS as being the UCS in which the selected entity was originally defined.
- View: defines the UCS as parallel with the current view.
- X/Y/Z: rotates the current UCS about its existing axes.
- Prev: restores the previously defined UCS. This can be repeated for up to ten UCS's.
- Restore: restores a saved UCS.
- Save: saves the current UCS.
- Delete: deletes a saved UCS.
- ?: lists the saved UCS's.
- World: the default, returns to the WCS.

UCSICON

- controls the display and position of the UCS icon

Command Sequence

Command: **UCSICON**
→ **SETTINGS** → **next** → **UCSICON:**
↓ **Settings** → **UCS** → **Icon▸**

Command Options

In Modelspace, the X and Y directions are shown by the arrows. In Paperspace, the apices of a triangle show the directions. The direction of the Z-axis is also indicated. A box is drawn at the bottom of the icon if it is being viewed from the positive Z-direction. A cross is shown at the bottom of the icon if it is located at the origin of the current UCS. And, if the current UCS coincides with the WCS, a W is added just above the cross. If the current view direction is along an edge of the UCS (or very nearly so), the icon is a broken pencil to show that pointing to objects on the screen is inadvisable.

The prompts are: ON/OFF/All/Noorigin/ORigin<ON>:.

ON and OFF determine whether or not the icon is displayed in the current viewport. All makes the settings apply to all viewports, not just the current one. Noorigin forces the icon to the bottom left of the display regardless of the position of the origin. ORigin places the icon at the origin of the UCS. which may well be off the screen..

If the system variable UCSICON is 1, the UCS icon is displayed. If it is 2, then the icon is displayed at the origin.

VIEW/DDVIEW*

- saves views of a drawing

Command Sequence

Command: **VIEW**
→ **DISPLAY** → **VIEW**
↓ **View** → **Set View** → **Named View...**
'VIEW

Command Options

The prompt is: ?/Delete/Restore/Save/Window:. The ? option lists all the view names. Delete can be used to delete unwanted views. If Restore is selected, then a view name is input and that view displayed in the current viewport. Save allows a view to be named and saved. Window is used if only part of the current viewport is to be saved. The window is defined by picking two diagonally opposite corners of the rectangular window.

If a view created in Paperspace is restored while Modelspace is in effect, a switch is made to Paperspace.

DDVIEW performs the same operations as VIEW but uses a dialogue box.

VPOINT

- sets a viewpoint in 3D space

Command Sequence

Command: **VPOINT**

→ DISPLAY → VPOINT:

↓ View → Set View → Viewpoint

Command Options

The prompt: Rotate/<Viewpoint>: is displayed. If the Rotate option is selected, two angles are needed in response to the prompts:

Enter angle in X-Y plane from X axis:

Enter angle from X-Y plane:

The two angles are sometimes called Azimuth and Elevation.

If RETURN is entered after the first prompt so that the default option Viewpoint is selected, a compass and axis tripod display results. The compass is the two concentric circles shown at the upper right corner of the screen. The viewpoint can be set in three-dimensions using this compass. The centre of the circles represents a view looking down on the model from the direction (0, 0, 1). The outside circle represents a view looking up at the model from the direction (0, 0, -1). Intermediate views may also be set, the inner circle representing a view looking at the model from the direction (X, X, 0). The crosshair may be moved to anywhere in the circle and a direction of sight defined.

To aid in visualising the rotation, an axis tripod is shown. This is a representation of the local X, Y and Z axes.

VPORTS/VIEWPORTS
- manages multiple viewports

Command Sequence

Command: **VPORTS/VIEWPORTS**
→ SETTINGS → next → VPORTS:

Command Options

VPORTS and VIEWPORTS are identical commands. They are only used within Modelspace. TILEMODE must be set to 1 for VPORTS to be available. The views set up by VPORTS are associative, all views changing to reflect changes in the drawing. Only one viewport can be current at a time - it is distinguished by a thicker border. Viewports are non-overlapping (or "tiled"). The current viewport may be switched by clicking inside a new viewport. When the pointing device is in the current viewport, its position is shown by crosshairs; in a non-current viewport, its position is shown by an arrow.

Viewports can contain any type of view of the drawing. One might contain a perspective view, another a plan view. Each viewport has its own virtual display so that panning and zooming may be done in the active viewport without affecting the others.

Save/Restore/Delete/Join/Single/?/2/<3>/4: is the prompt on receipt of the command.

Save: saves the current viewport configuration. A list of currently saved viewports may be displayed. The viewport name is then typed and may be up to 31 characters long.

Restore: is used to restore a viewport configuration.

Delete: is used to delete a viewport configuration.

Join: is used to merge two adjacent viewports into one. The new viewport must be rectangular. One is defined as the dominant viewport and the other selected to join it, the new, merged viewport taking the settings of the dominant viewport.

Single: changes the display configuration to a single viewport. The view shown in the current viewport is drawn in the merged viewport which takes its settings also.

?: lists saved viewport configurations.

2: divides the display into two viewports. The division may be horizontal or vertical.

3: divides the display into three viewports. The configuration is set from Horizontal/Vertical/Above/Below/Left/<Right>:. Horizontal and Vertical divide the display into three equally sized viewports. The other options result in one large viewport and two smaller ones of equal size. The option describes the position of the large viewport.

4: divides the display into four viewports.

System variables connected with VPORTS are: CVPORT, MAXACTVP, TILEMODE, VSMAX and VSMIN.

ZOOM

- zooms into and out of the drawing

Command Sequence

Command: **ZOOM**
→ DISPLAY → ZOOM:
↓ View → ZOOM
'ZOOM (Release 12 only)

Command Options

All/Center/Dynamic/Extents/Left/Previous/Vmax/Window/<Scale (X/XP)>: is the main prompt displayed.

- All: results in a zoom to the larger of the drawing's limits or extents.
- Center: gives a zoom centred on a specific point and of a defined magnification. The centre point is picked and the prompt: Magnification or Height: is received. The height may be input (in drawing units) or a magnification factor. A magnification value less than one will zoom out of the screen. If the magnification number is followed by X, the magnification is taken as a factor of the current magnification. XP after the magnification scales the drawing relative to Paperspace.

- Dynamic: displays the virtual screen and allows the use of a view box. The drawing extents, current view and virtual screen are shown as a white box, a dotted green box and red corner marks on colour displays. A box containing a cross is the dynamic view box. This can be panned, enlarged or shrunk using the cursor. When the view box is the right size, RETURN is pressed and the new view displayed. If the view requires a regeneration, an hourglass is shown in the corner of the screen.
- Extents: displays a view of the whole drawing which is drawn as large as possible within the drawing area.
- Left: requires the bottom left corner point but apart from that works like Center.
- Previous: displays the view last created by a ZOOM, PAN or VIEW command. Up to ten views are saved for each viewport.
- Vmax: creates the largest view that will not cause a regeneration.
- Window: zooms a rectangular area based on a picked window. In Release 12, if a point is defined, the Zoom takes this option automatically.
- Scale(X): magnifies the drawing relative to the drawing limits. If the scale factor is followed by X, the scale factor is relative to the current view.
- Scale(XP): magnifies the view in relation to Paperspace.

5 Annotation & Hatching

ASCTEXT

- imports an ASCII file into a drawing

Command Sequence

Command: **ASCTEXT**

↓ **Draw →Text → Import Text**

Command Options

ASCTEXT is not an AutoCAD command. It is an AutoLISP function useful for placing long text passages on a drawing. The text may be conveniently generated in an external program, for instance a wordprocessor, and exported as an ASCII (American Standard Code for Information Interchange) file. This type of file contains no formatting information so ASCTEXT provides options for formatting it inside AutoCAD. The text style should be set up before the text is imported.

- Filetoread (including extension) <default>:. The file name is supplied. If the system variable FILEDIA is set to 1, the File Read dialogue box is used to enter the filename rather than entering it at the prompt.
- Start point or Center/Middle/Right/?:. The point at which the text begins on the drawing should be picked. Alternatively, a justification option may be input. A list of the possible options is obtained on input of ?. These are listed in this section under the command TEXT.
- Height <default>:. The text height is specified.
- Rotation Angle <0>:. The text rotation angle is specified.
- Change text options? <N>:. This determines how the text is placed in the drawing. If N (or RETURN) is entered, the text is drawn at the default setting. Otherwise, a string of prompts is issued so that the form of the text may be specified. These follow.
    - Distance between lines/<Auto>:
    - First line to read/<1>:
    - Number of lines to read <All>:
    - Underscore each line? <N>:
    - Overscore each line ? <N>:
    - Change text case? Upper/Lower/ <N>:
    - Set up columns? <N>:

- Distance between columns: } If Y is
- Number of lines per column: } returned

BHATCH*
- hatches a region by picking an internal point

Command Sequence
Command: **BHATCH**
→ **DRAW** → **BHATCH:**
↓ **Draw** → **Hatch...**

Command Options
In BHATCH, a closed boundary polyline is created around the hatch region. This may be discarded after the hatch is finished. The Boundary Hatch dialogue box is displayed.

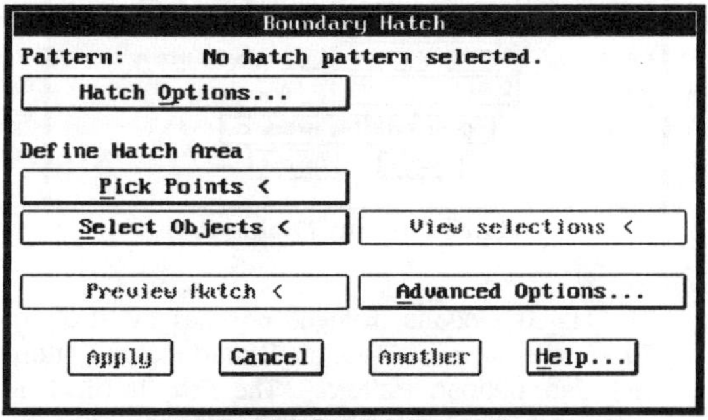

5.1 BHATCH Dialogue Box

This permits the definition of the hatch pattern required with its angle and scale. There is also an extensive set of options determining how the hatch is to be carried out. A very useful facility is the previewing of hatches before they are finalised. Also, user-defined hatch patterns may be designed. The Boundary Hatch dialogue box has ten buttons. Three of these may be used to display secondary dialogue boxes.

- Hatch Options. Clicking this button displays the Hatch Options dialogue box.
- Pick Points. Clicking this button allows points inside the hatch areas to be picked.
- Select Objects. Clicking this button permits boundary

objects to be selected.

- View Selection. Clicking this button results in the objects selected for boundary estimation to be highlighted.
- Preview Hatch. Clicking this button results in the display of the hatch as it would appear if current settings were maintained.
- Advanced Options. Clicking this button displays the Advanced Options dialogue box.
- Apply. Clicking this button results in the hatch being done with the current settings.
- Another. Clicking this button results in the Boundary Hatch dialogue box being redisplayed so that further hatching can be done.

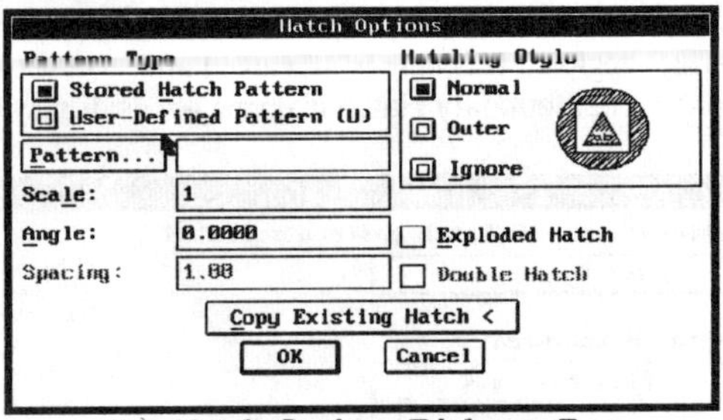

5.2 Hatch Options Dialogue Box

The Hatch Options dialogue box has two Pattern Type radio buttons. These are Stored Hatch Pattern and User-defined Pattern. The first, if filled in, specifies that the hatch pattern to be used has previously been stored on the disk. The Spacing box and Double Hatch check box are grayed out. The User-defined Pattern button, if filled in, permits the definition of simple customised hatched or cross-hatched patterns. The Spacing box and Double Hatch check box are then enabled. There are various other elements in the dialogue box.

- Pattern... Clicking this button results in the Choose Hatch Pattern dialogue box being displayed. This contains samples of the sixty standard hatch patterns supplied with AutoCAD. The samples can be paged through by using the Previous and Next buttons. A hatch may be selected by picking its picture. Each hatch pattern has a name (eg ANSI31) and if this is known, it can be entered directly.

- Scale. Each hatch pattern is stored in a standard size. A scale factor may be typed in the Scale box. This is a numerical value, possibly a decimal fraction, by which the hatch pattern will be scaled before drawing. A number less than one will result in a pattern with features closer together.
- Angle. Each hatch pattern is stored in a standard orientation. A rotation angle may be typed in the Angle box.
- Spacing. The distance between hatch lines may be typed in this box for user-defined hatch patterns.
- Hatching Style. This box contains three options. When one is picked, a picture shows its action.
  - Normal Style hatches alternate areas within the hatch boundary.
  - Outer Style hatches only the outermost area.
  - Ignore Style hatches from the hatch boundary ignoring any islands in the middle.
- Exploded Hatch. Normally, the elements of a hatch may not be edited; a hatch is an entity. This option explodes the hatch so that it can be treated as a set of separate entities.
- Double Hatch. The user-defined pattern is mirrored to produce cross-hatching.
- Copy Existing Hatch. Clicking this button enables the selection of a hatch using the current settings.

The Advanced Options dialogue box contains three options.

- Define Boundary Set. The Make New Boundary Set button enables the picking of displayed entities to form a new boundary set. The From Everything on Screen radio button results in all displayed entities to be considered for the boundary formation. The From Existing Boundary Set causes an existing boundary set to be modified by adding and subtracting entities.
- Ray Casting. This scrolled list box allows the first search direction for finding a possible boundary to be selected. Options are +/-X, +/-Y.
- Retain Boundaries. This check box permits the retention of the calculated boundary as a closed polyline.

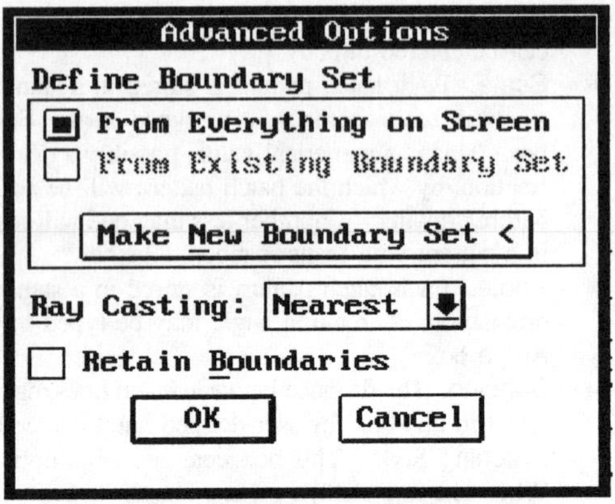

5.3 Advanced Options Dialogue Box

DDEDIT

- provides a dialogue box for editing text

Command Sequence

Command: **DDEDIT**
→ **EDIT** → **DDEDIT:**

Command Options

The prompt <Select a TEXT or ATTDEF object>/Undo: is displayed. When the text is picked, a dialogue box appears containing that text. Text may be edited by moving the cursor with the mouse, using BACKSPACE and DELETE to remove text, and typing new text at the cursor position. When the text has been successfully edited, clicking on OK exits DDEDIT. Entering U removes the effect of the edit.

DTEXT

- adds text dynamically

Command Sequence

Command: **DTEXT**
→ **DRAW** → **DTEXT:**
↓ **Draw** → **Text** → **Dynamic**

Command Options

Besides the facility of text being drawn while it is being typed, DTEXT has other advantages over the TEXT command. DTEXT allows multiple lines to be drawn, possibly at arbitrary points on the display, and without leaving the command.

The first prompt is Justify/Style/<Start point>:.

The default option can be chosen by picking the point at which the text is to begin - this is known as "left justification". The text may then be typed and will be shown on the screen as it is being entered. At the final RETURN it is possible to enter a new line of text which will be placed immediately under the last unless a new start point is picked. The command is left when a RETURN is entered at the Text: prompt.

A new current text style may be selected by selecting the Style option. In this case, the style, which must have been previously defined using the STYLE command, will be supplied and the height and angle defined in response the the Height: and Rotation angle: prompts.

The text can be arranged around a start point in ways other than left justification by choosing the Justify option. This provides a comprehensive range of justifications.

- Align. The start and endpoint of the text are specified and the text is fitted between them, its height and width being adjusted to suit the space for the text.
- Fit. The start, endpoint and text height are specified and the text width is adjusted so that the text fits into the space available.
- Center. The text is spaced equally about the point picked with its base line at the same vertical height as the point.
- Middle. The text is spaced equally about the point picked in an horizontal and a vertical direction.
- Right. The text is right justified. The right hand side of the text is placed flush with the picked point with its base line at the same vertical height as the point.
- There are another nine justification options. These are systematically coded with two letters:

T: Top	M: Middle	B: Bottom
L: Left	C: Center	R: Right

These positional codes refer to a box completely bounding the text. The text is placed relative to the picked datum point as follows:

TL	TC	TR
ML	MC	MR
BL	BC	BR

The bounding box height is based on a text character with both ascenders and descenders. Figure 5.8 shows the types of justification.

HATCH
- hatches a closed region of the drawing

Command Sequence

Command: **HATCH**
→ **DRAW** → **HATCH:**
↓ **Draw** → **Hatch**

Command Options

Hatching is notoriously a tricky process in any CAD system. Bad hatches can result from superposed lines and tiny gaps in the drawing. Both of these are difficult to detect on the graphical display. The Release 12 BHATCH command gives better control over hatching than the older HATCH, mainly because the hatch can be previewed.

The first prompt is Pattern(? or name/U, style)<default>:. One of AutoCAD's many supplied hatch pattern names may be typed, if it is known. A list of these can be displayed by typing ?. The default is the current hatch pattern.

Alternatively, a simple cross-hatched pattern can be user-defined by selecting the U option.

If ? is selected, the prompt Pattern(s) to list <*>: will be given. A subset of the available patterns may be obtained by using the wildcards * and ?. The default option shows all pattern names. Following this, a valid pattern name is selected. The patterns provided are stored at a standard scale and orientation angle. If these are unsatisfactory, a new scale and angle may be provided after the prompts: Scale for pattern <1>: and Angle for pattern:.

If the option U is chosen, the user will be asked for the

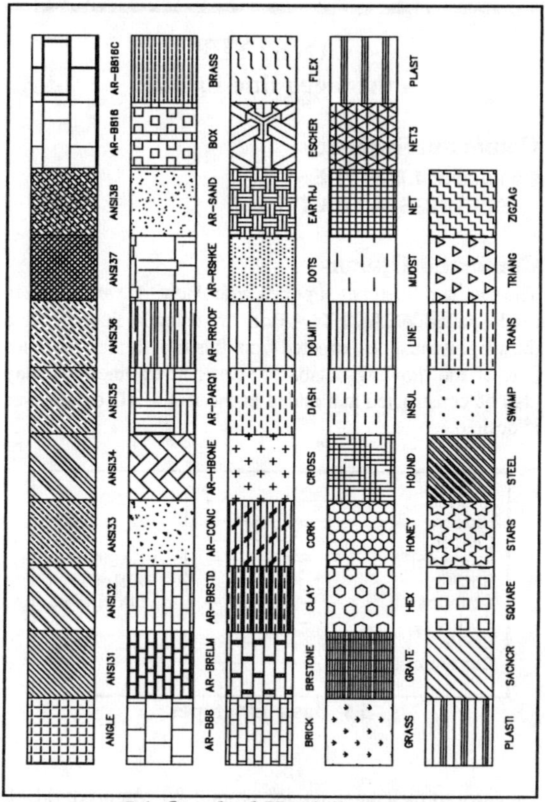

5.4 Standard Hatch Patterns

angle for the hatchlines, the spacing (in drawing units) between the lines and whether double hatching is required. If double hatching is chosen, a second set of lines perpendicular to those already defined will be added to the pattern.

Finally, the prompt Select objects: will be given. The entities making up the hatch boundary will be picked. For complex boundaries, it is often necessary to do some preparatory work before the HATCH command is given. This usually involves breaking lines and adding bounding polylines.

LINETYPE
- manages line formats

Command Sequence

Command: **LINETYPE**
→ **SETTINGS** → **LINETYP:**

Command Options

The standard linetypes supplied with AutoCAD are stored in a file called ACAD.LIN. Prior to using a linetype in a drawing, it must be extracted from this file. It then becomes part of the drawing database. Customised linetypes may also be constructed and added to the AutoCAD definitions, if desired.

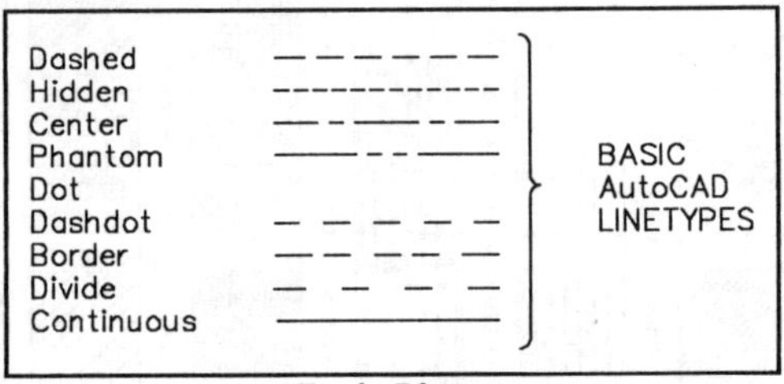

5.5 Basic Linetypes

On entry to the command, the prompt ?/Create/Load/Set: is presented.

- ? This option allows all available linetypes to be listed. Not only can the linetypes in ACAD.LIN be listed but also linetypes stored in any other file with the extension LIN. The prompt is File to list <ACAD>:.
- Create This option is taken when a customised linetype is to be defined. A linetype name (up to 31 characters with no spaces) is entered in response to the prompt: Name of linetype to create:. The new linetype may be added to those already defined in ACAD.LIN, or another file with extension LIN can be created to hold it. This is done using the Create or Append Linetype File dialogue box.

The new linetype must next be described. This is done by first entering a line of text which will be used to show the linetype form when it is listed. This is entered in response to the prompt: Creating new file...Descriptive text: and is a string of up to 47 characters, including spaces, dashes, full stops and underscores. This is not the definition; it is just a crude representation of the linetype.
The linetype is now defined after the prompt: Enter pattern (on next line):. A list of numbers is entered separated by commas. A negative number indicates that number of spaces, a zero indicates a dot and a positive number indicates that number of line segments. The numbers need not be integers. The list represents one cycle of the new linetype.

- Load — A prompt is displayed: Linetype(s) to load: A linetype name is input or, if this is not known, RETURN may be typed which results in the display of the Select Linetype File dialogue box. This shows all the AutoCAD linetypes from which a selection may be made. If the name provided is the name of a linetype already loaded, a message is displayed.
- Set — New entity linetype <default>: is displayed and is answered by the name of a linetype already loaded. This will become the current linetype and all subsequent entities will be drawn using it. Linetypes can be assigned to layers. If the name BYLAYER is entered, subsequent entities will be drawn in the linetype of their layer.

LTSCALE
- scales linetypes

Command Sequence
Command: **LTSCALE**
→ **SETTINGS** → **next** → **LTSCALE:**

Command Options
Linetypes are stored by AutoCAD to a standard scale. This is usually unsuitable for the scale of the drawing. This

command rescales the linetypes. It has one prompt only: New scale factor <1>:. The scale factor is input as a number and it may need some trial and error before a satisfactory result is achieved. The current scale is held in a system variable LTSCALE. System variable PSLTSCALE holds the scale value for linetypes in paper scale.

QTEXT
- draws a box instead of text

Command Sequence
Command: **QTEXT**
→ **SETTINGS** → **next** → **QTEXT**

Command Options
Many drawings contain a lot of annotation and since text has to be drawn, regeneration can take a long time. The command QTEXT results in bounding boxes being drawn instead of the text characters which speeds things up. The prompt is ON/OFF:.

STYLE
- loads and makes current a text style

Command Sequence
Command: **STYLE**
→ **SETTINGS** → **next** → **STYLE:**

Command Options
AutoCAD provides twenty standard text fonts. Each of these may be used to generate a style, which has its own width, height and obliquing angle. The style may also have directional characteristics: backwards, upside-down and vertical. Each font has a name (eg ROMAND for Duplex Roman) and each style using it should also have a user-provided name. The prompts are:

- Text style name (or ?) <current style>:. A style name should be provided. If, instead, ? is returned, a list of currently defined styles is provided. The list can contain all the currently defined styles or a subset of them if a wildcard name is given in reply to the prompt:

Text style(s) to list <*>: If RETURN is input, the style name will take the font name by default. The Select Font File dialogue box is displayed. This shows all the file names that contain the fonts. One should be selected and its name will then appear in the File: box.

- A string of prompts appear for setting the various style characteristics.
  - Height <0.0>:
  - Width factor <1.0>:
  - Obliquing angle <0>:
  - Backwards ?<N>:
  - Upside-down ?<N>:
  - Vertical ? <N>:

A message will then appear stating that the style is current. The Height <0.0>: option may appear strange at first sight. A height of 0.0 is interpreted to mean that the height will be asked for when the style is being used in commands such as TEXT.

SIMPLEX FONT ROMANS	TRIPLEX FONT ROMANT
DUPLEX FONT ROMAND	GOTHIC FONT GOTHICE
COMPLEX FONT ROMANC	LOTS OF OTHERS TOO

5.6 Some Text Styles

TEXT
- adds text to a drawing

Command Sequence
Command: **TEXT:**
→ **DRAW** → **next** → **TEXT:**

Command Options
Unlike DTEXT, TEXT only permits the drawing of one line of text. However, if the command is re-entered (if immediately, by RETURN), the cursor will be placed on the line just below the last line of text drawn.

The first prompt is Justify/Style/<Start point>:.

- The default option can be chosen by picking the point

at which the text is to begin - this is known as "left justification". The text may then be typed and will be shown on the screen as it is being entered. At the final RETURN it is possible to enter a new line of text which will be placed immediately under the last unless a new start point is picked.

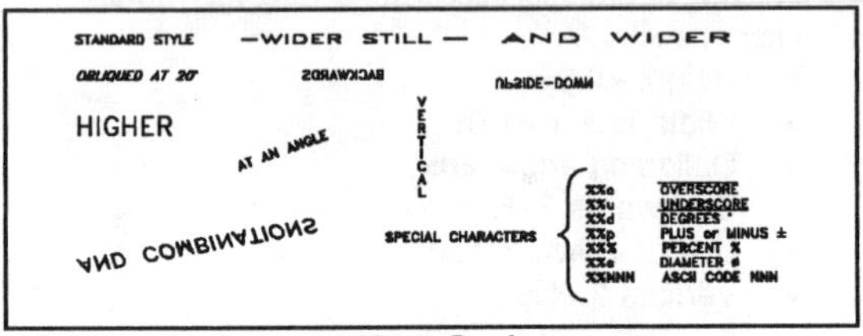

5.7 Text Options

- A new current text style may be selected by selecting the Style option. In this case, the style, which must have been previously defined using the STYLE command, will be supplied and the height and angle defined in response to the Height: and Rotation angle: prompts.
- The text can be arranged around a start point in ways other than left justification by choosing the Justify option. This provides a comprehensive range of justifications.
  - Align. The start and endpoint of the text are specified and the text is fitted between them, its height and width being adjusted to suit the space for the text.
  - Fit. The start, endpoint and text height are specified and the text is fitted between the start and endpoint. In this case, the text width is adjusted to suit the space available.
  - Center. The text is spaced equally about the point picked with its base line at the same vertical height as the point.
  - Middle. The text is spaced equally about the point picked in an horizontal and a vertical direction.
  - Right. The text is right justified. The right hand side of the text is placed flush with the picked point with its base line at the same vertical height as the point.

  - There are another nine justification options. These

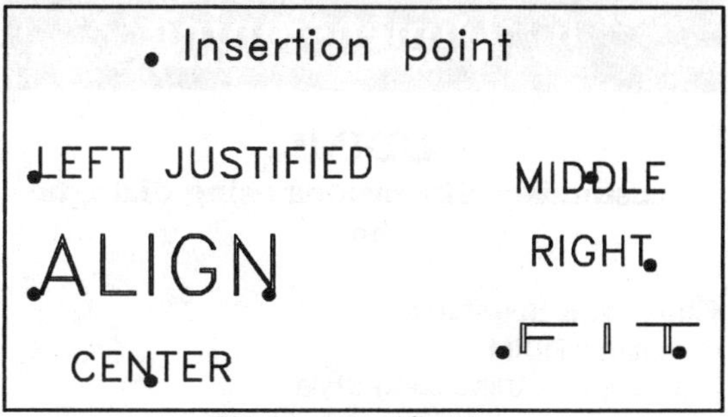

5.8 Text Justification

are systematically coded with two letters:

T: Top	M: Middle	B: Bottom
L: Left	C: Center	R: Right

These positional codes refer to a box completely bounding the text. The text is placed relative to the picked datum point as follows:

TL	TC	TR
ML	MC	MR
BL	BC	BR

The bounding box height is based on a text character with both ascenders and descenders.

Special characters, specialised to drafting, can be inserted into text strings using the escape codes %%.

%%c	diameter symbol ϕ	%%o	overscore toggle
%%d	degrees symbol	%%u	underscore toggle
%%p	plus/minus ±	%%%	percent symbol

6 Dimensioning

DDIM*

- customises dimensions using dialogue box

Command Sequence

Command: **DDIM**

↓ Settings → Dimension Style...

Command Options

The dialogue box enables all the system variables used in the command DIM to be set in a convenient way. The DDIM box has six subsidiary dialogue boxes which may be used to set:

- Dimension lines
- Extension lines
- Arrows
- Text location
- Text format
- Dimension colours.

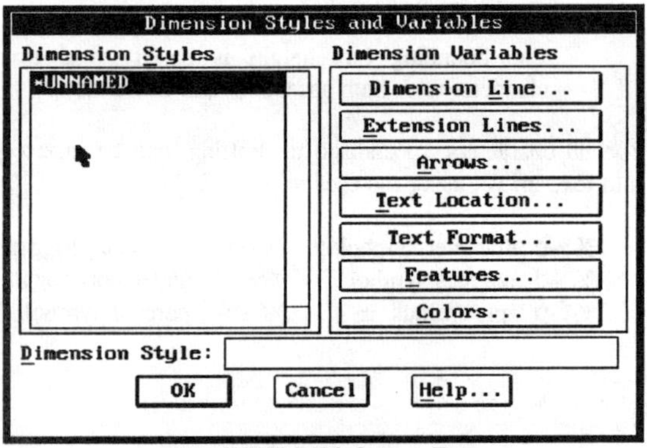

6.1 DDIM Dialogue Box

Dimension variables which may be adjusted in this way are:

- Associative dimensioning: DIMASO, DIMSHO.
- Scaling dimensions: DIMSCALE, DIMTXT, DIMASZ, DIMTSZ, DIMCEN, DIMLFAC.
- Dimension & extension line offsets: DIMEXO, DIMEXE, DIMDLI, DIMDLE.

- Form of toleranced dimensions: DIMTP, DIMTM, DIMTOL, DIMLIM.
- Rounding of dimensions: DIMRND, DIMZIN.
- Dimension text controls: DIMGAP, DIMTFAC, DIMTIH, DIMTOH, DIMTAD, DIMTIX, DIMTVP.
- Control of extension lines: DIMSE1, DIMSE2, DIMTOFL, DIMSOXD.
- Colours: DIMCLRD, DIMCLRE, DIMCLRT.
- Alternative dimensions: DIMALT, DIMALTF, DIMALTD, DIMPOST, DIMAPOST, DIMBLK, DIMSAH, DIMBLK1, DIMBLK2, DIMSTYLE.

For explanation of the action of these system variables, see Section 12: System Variables. They may also be set by returning their names to the Command: prompt.

DIM

- adds dimensions to drawings

Command Sequence

Command: **DIM**

↓ **Draw** → **Dimensions▸**

Command Options

DIM is a subsystem with its own command line prompt. It is entered by using the command DIM and exited by using Exit.

Some of its commands are identical with those found in the main system but have a different action. There are 27 options in the AutoCAD DIM system. These are:

Aligned	Leader	Save
Angular	Newtext	Status
Baseline	Oblique	Style
Center	Ordinate	Tedit
Continue	Override	Trotate
Diameter	Radius	Undo
Exit	Redraw	Update
Hometext	Restore	Variables
Horizontal	Rotated	Vertical

DIM:ALigned
- aligns a dimension line with a feature

Command Sequence

DIM: **Aligned**
↓ **Draw** → **Dimensions▸** → **Linear▸** → **Aligned**

Command Options

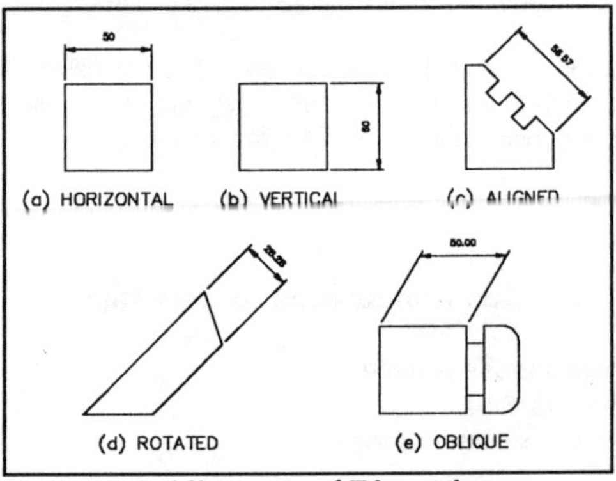

6.2 Alignment of Dimensions

The following sequence will be presented:

- First extension line origin or RETURN to select: If a point on the feature is picked, the system will demand the Second extension line origin: This will define the angle at which the dimension line is to be drawn. If RETURN is entered, AutoCAD will make a reasoned guess using the second pick point as a clue to what is intended. In this case, another prompt will be issued: Select line, arc or circle: If a line, arc or polyline segment is picked, the extension line origins are assumed to be the endpoints. If a circle is chosen, another extension line origin, diametrically opposite to the first, will be assumed.
- Dimension line location (Text/Angle): If a point is picked, the dimension line will be drawn through that point. The dimension text will be shown in the current drawing units and decimal places. This may be overridden by entering any desired text. Alternatively, either Text or Angle may be chosen. In the first case,

the default dimension text, to the currently drawing units and precision will be displayed. This may be overridden. In the second case, the angle at which the text is to be drawn may be defined.

DIM:ANgular
- dimensions angles

Command Sequence

DIM: **Angular**

↓ **Draw** → **Dimensions▸** → **Angular**

Command Options

The following option sequence will be presented:

Select arc, circle, line or RETURN:

What follows depends on the input. If RETURN is chosen, the system assumes that the angle between three points is intended. The three points will in the order: Angle vertex:, First angle endpoint:, Second angle endpoint:.

- If an arc is picked, the angle subtended by the arc will be assumed.
- If a line is picked, the dimension between that line and a second line will be assumed. A prompt Second line: will be issued.
- If a circle is picked, the pick point is taken as the first extension origin and a prompt Second angle end point: will be issued.

In all cases, Dimension arc location (Text/Angle): will follow. The point picked is of particular importance, since the system takes this position as a hint to which angle should be dimensioned. For instance, in the arc option, two angles are possible: theacute or the obtuse angle. The position selected should determine which of the two is to be dimensioned.

Either Text or Angle may be chosen. In the first case, the default dimension text, to the currently drawing units and precision will be displayed. This may be overridden. In the second case, the angle at which the text is to be drawn may be defined.

DIM:Baseline
- draws linear dimensions to a baseline

Command Sequence

DIM: **next BASELINE**

↓ **Draw → Dimensions▸ → Linear → Baseline**

Command Options

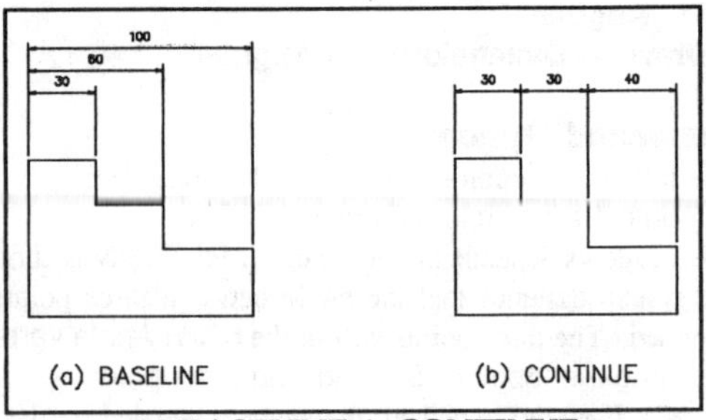

6.3 BASELINE & CONTINUE

The BASELINE option draws one or more linear dimensions using the first extension line of an existing linear dimension as datum. This existing extension line will be used as the first extension line of the baseline dimensions but will be extended appropriately.

- If the last dimension drawn was a linear one, the prompt Second extension line origin or RETURN to select: will be issued. If a second extension line origin is picked, the new linear dimension will be drawn with its dimension line offset from that of the existing dimension at an amount set by the system variable DIMDLI. The process may be repeated.
- If RETURN is typed in response to the prompt, or if the last dimension created was not linear, a base dimension must be chosen in response to the prompt Select base dimension:. The extension line closest to the pick point will be taken as the datum.
- In either of the previous cases, the dimension text will then be displayed in the current format. This may be overridden.

DIM:CEnter

- draws centre lines and marks

Command Sequence

DIM: → **next** → **CEnter**

↓ **Draw** → **Dimensions▸** → **Radial▸ Center Mark**

Command Options

This option places centrelines or centre marks on arcs, circles or arc segments of polylines. The prompt Select arc or circle: is issued. The form of the resulting centreline is influenced by the system variable DIMCEN.

- If DIMCEN is O, no centrelines will be drawn.
- If DIMCEN has a positive value, the mark lengths will be twice that value.
- If DIMCEN has a negative value, the mark lengths will extend beyond the circle or arc, the extra length being the absolute value of DIMCEN.

DIM:COntinue

- chains linear dimensions

Command Sequence

DIM: **next** **Continue**

↓ **Draw** → **Dimensions▸** → **Linear▸** → **Continue**

Command Options

This option performs the chaining of dimensions, the second extension line of one dimension being used as the first extension line of the next - see Figure 6.3. The command can be repeated to obtain a series of end-to-end dimensions.

- Upon receiving the command, the system returns: Second extension line origin or RETURN to select:, if the previous dimension created is linear.
- If RETURN is entered, or the last dimension created is not linear, the prompt: Select continued dimension: is displayed and a new extension line can be picked. This will act as the first extension line of the continued dimension.
- Finally, the dimension text will be displayed in the format currently set. This can be replaced by any input text if required.

DIM:Diameter

- dimensions arcs and circles

Command Sequence

DIM: **Diameter**

↓ **Draw** → **Dimensions▸** → **Radial▸** → **Diameter**

Command Options

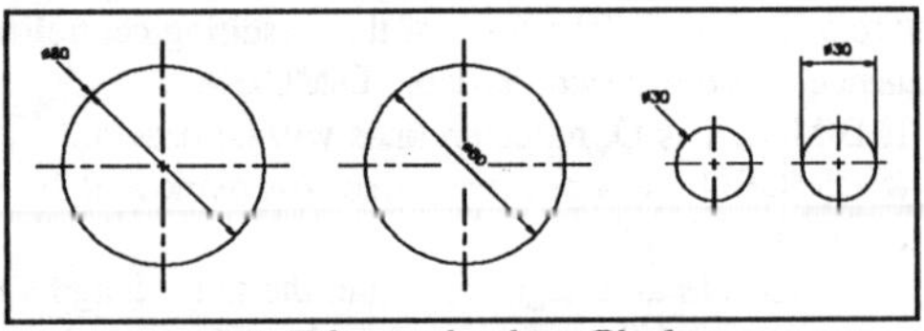

6.4 Dimensioning Circles

The first prompt is Select arc or circle: The position of the pick point on the arc, circle or polyline arc segment is important since the dimension line will pass through it.

The dimension text will then be displayed. This is the measured size, preceded by the special character %%c (which is equivalent to ϕ, the conventional symbol for diameter). This default text may be overridden.

The form of the dimension is determined by several dimension variables.

- If DIMTIX (Text inside extension lines) is set to 1, the dimension text will be placed inside the extension lines. If it is set to 0, the text will be placed outside them.
- If DIMTOFL (Text outside, force dimension line inside) is set to 1 and DIMTIX is set to 0, dimension text will be placed outside the circle or arc.
- If both DIMTIX and DIMTOFL are set to 0, a leader line will be added from the dimension text to the pick point. The position of the text end of the leader line can be set by dragging the line to a desired position. In this case, another prompt is displayed. This is Enter leader line length for text:. If RETURN is entered, a default (minimum) length is provided.

- If DIMCEN is non-zero, centre lines will be drawn. The effect of various settings of DIMCEN is described in DIM: CEnter in this section.

DIM:Exit
- quits the dimensioning sub-system

Command Sequence
DIM: **Exit**

Command Options
This command has no options. The user is returned to the normal command prompt.

DIM:HOMetext
- restores text to default position

Command Sequence
DIM: **Edit HOMETEXT**
↓ **Modify → Edit Dims▸ → Dimension Text▸ → Home Position**

Command Options
This option is used to restore associative dimension texts to their default positions after they have been moved by editing commands such as STRETCH & TROTATE. The command issues just one prompt: Select Objects: The dimensions are then selected and the text restored to the default position.

DIM:HORizontal
- dimensions horizontally

Command Sequence
DIM: **Horizntl**
↓ **Draw → Dimensions▸ → Linear▸ → Horizontal**

Command Options
The first prompt is First extension line origin or RETURN to Select.:

- If a point is selected, then the prompt: Second

extension line origin: will be issued. The second point defining the extents of the dimension may then be selected.

- If RETURN is entered to the first prompt, the prompt Select line, arc or circle: will appear. When the entity is selected, the extension line origins will be defined automatically at its ends.

In either case, the prompt Dimension line location (Text/Angle): will be displayed. A point at which the dimension line is to pass may be picked. The Text and Angle options may be used to modify the default text and to set the dimension text to a desired angle.
The dimension will be drawn with extension lines vertical and dimension line horizontal. The feature itself need not be horizontal. See Figure 6.2.

DIM:Leader
- draws leader lines with text

Command Sequence
DIM: **Leader**
↓ **Draw → Dimensions▸ → Leader**

Command Options
The option draws a leader line with a pointing marker (normally an arrow) on one end and some text on the other.

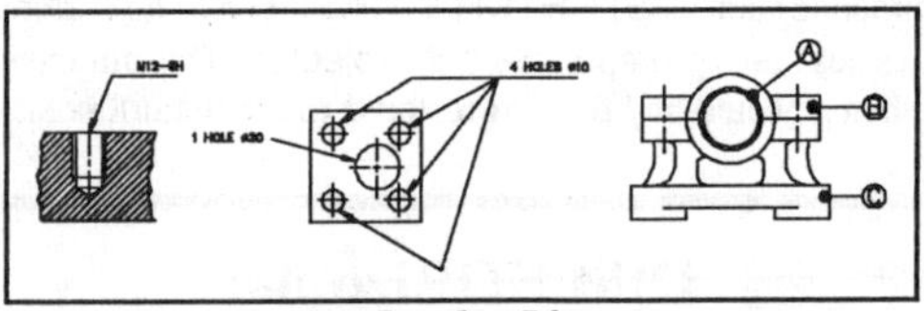

6.5 Leader Lines

The prompt Leader start: will be returned. The point at which the leader line arrow is to be placed should be picked.

To point: may be used repeatedly to form a leader with several line segments. These may be positioned interactively using rubber-banding. If a segment is entered in error, it may be deleted by entering U at the next To point: prompt. RETURN terminates the chain of line segments. If the last segment is not within 15° from the horizontal, a single horizontal line segment, one arrow length, is added at the end of the chain. The arrow size may be adjusted by setting the dimension variable DIMASZ.

Finally, the text to be added at the end of the leader line may be typed. The command can only cope with single line text; if more than one line is needed, it must be added to the leader using the normal TEXT or DTEXT commands, entering SPACE at the prompt for leader text.

DIM:Newtext
- changes dimension text.

Command Sequence

DIM: **Edit Newtext**

↓ **Modify → Edit Dims → Dimension Text → Change Text**

Command Options

This option is used only on associative dimensions. The new text is typed in response to the prompt: Enter new dimension text:. Existing text may be removed completely by entering SPACE. Or text may be restored to its default string by entering RETURN. The dimensions to be modified are then selected in answer to Select objects:.

DIM:OBlique
- makes extension lines oblique to dimension lines

Command Sequence

DIM: **OBLIQUE**

↓ **Modify → Edit Dims▸ → Dimension Text▸ → Oblique Dimension**

Command Options

Normally, the extension lines are at right-angles to the dimension lines but, occasionally, in a closely detailed drawing, it is useful to draw them at some other angle - see Figure 6.2. The dimensions to be modified are selected in response to the prompt: Select Objects:. Only associative dimensions may be selected. An obliquing angle is entered

after the prompt Enter obliquing angle (RETURN for none):. This follows the normal convention that positive angles are anticlockwise unless this convention has been changed using the UNITS or DDUNITS commands.
Note that the dimension line and dimension text of an obliqued dimension does not change. Only the extension lines are rotated.

DIM:ORdinate
- draws dimensions from a datum

Command Sequence

DIM: **Ordinate**

↓ **Draw** → **Dimensions▸** → **Ordinate▸** → **Automatic**

Command Options

Ordinate dimensions have a leader line without a marker pointing to the feature of interest and dimension text showing the distance from a datum. The dimensions may be in X- or Y- direction on the current UCS. The required direction can be specified explicitly or can be determined by the point picked for location of the leader endpoint.

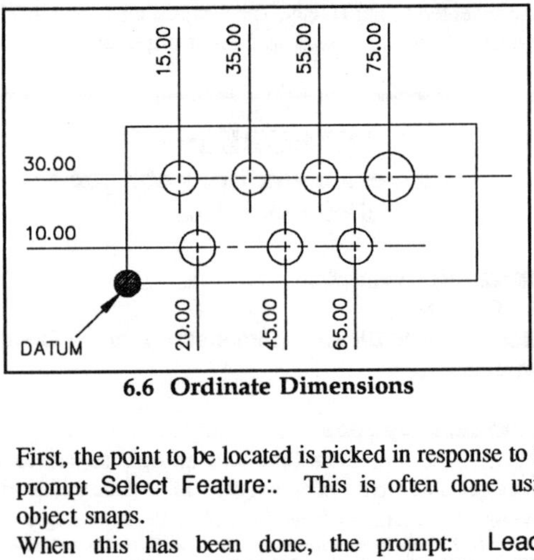

6.6 Ordinate Dimensions

- First, the point to be located is picked in response to the prompt Select Feature:. This is often done using object snaps.
- When this has been done, the prompt: Leader endpoint (Xdatum/Ydatum): appears. Either of the options Xdatum or Ydatum can be selected to define

the direction of the dimension lines explicitly. Alternatively, if the endpoint picked is closer to the X-axis than it is to the Y-axis, the X-direction is assumed by the system. Otherwise, the Y-direction is assumed.

- Finally, the dimension text must be defined. The default text is displayed in the current format. This can be overriden by user defined text. Text can be suppressed by typing SPACE.

DIM:OVerride
- modifies the appearance of selected dimensions

Command Sequence
DIM: **Dim Style Override**

Command Options
The option works by modifying selected dimension variables. The prompts are as follows:

- Dimension variable to override:. The name is entered. A list of the dimensions variables and a brief description of their action will be found in System Variables, Section 16.
- Current value <default> New value:. This, and the last, prompt will be repeated after each variable is entered. When all required variables have been adjusted, entering RETURN leads to the next prompt.
- Select objects:. The appropriate dimensions are selected. The newly defined settings are applied to them.
- Modify dimension style "current"? <N>:. If any of the selected dimensions have an associated named style, the named style can be updated by incorporating the new settings.

DIM:RAdius
- dimensions radii

Command Sequence
DIM: **Radius**

↓ **Draw** → **Dimensions>** → **Radial▸** → **Radius**

Command Options

This option may be used to dimension arcs, circles and arc segments of polylines. The form of dimension produced is dependent on the settings of several dimension variables.

If DIMTIX (Text inside extension lines) and DIMTOFL (Text outside, force dimension line inside) are both set to 0, a leader is drawn to the dimension text from the point picked on the entity to be dimensioned. If DIMTOFL is set to 1 and DIMTIX to 0, the text is placed outside the entity and a dimension line drawn from the centre of the arc or circle. The setting of DIMCEN influences whether centre marks are placed. If it is set to 0, no marks are drawn; if to a negative value, full centre lines are drawn extending beyond the curve to the absolute value of the setting. If the setting is positive, a small centre mark is drawn.

The first prompt is: Select arc or circle:. The point must be carefully picked, since its position will determine where the dimension line touches the entity to be dimensioned. After the entity has been selected, the user will be shown the default text. This will be prefixed by the letter R which is conventionally taken to mean "Radius" in most national standards. This dimension text can be overridden.

If DIMTIX is ON, the dimension text will appear outside the arc or circle. A leader line may be dragged to the text position in response to the prompt: Enter leader length for text:. Alternatively, a numerical length can be typed. Or, if RETURN is entered, the leader line will assume a default length.

DIM:REDraw

- redraws the current viewport

Command Sequence

DIM: **Redraw**

Command Options

There are no options. This works like the version of RESTORE in the main drawing editor.

DIM:REStore
- makes a named dimension style current

Command Sequence
DIM: **Dim Styl REStore**

Command Options
Current dimension style: <Name of current style> ?/Enter dimension style name or RETURN to select dimension: is displayed. The prompt shows the named style currently in force. If none is current, *UNNAMED is displayed.
If ? is returned, existing named styles will be listed.
If a style name is supplied, then that style will be made current.
If RETURN is entered, the prompt Select dimension: will be shown. An existing associative dimension should be selected. Its named setting will then be restored. If a tilde (~), is entered, the system will return a list of the differences between the current settings and the selected named style.

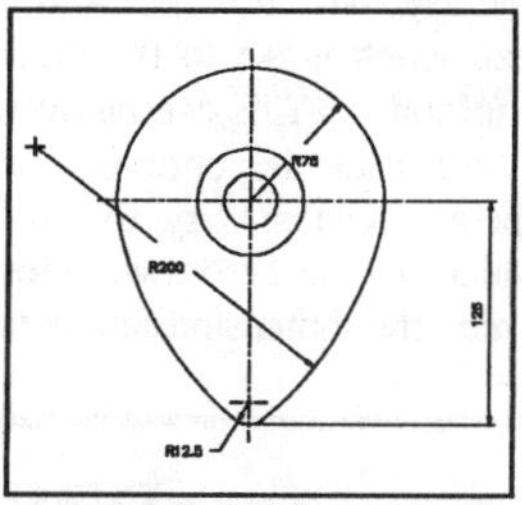

6.7 Radial Dimensions

DIM:ROtated
- draws a dimension line at an angle

Command Sequence
DIM: **ROTATED**
↓ **Draw → Dimensions▸ → Linear▸ → Rotated**

Command Options
The user will first be prompted for the angle at which the dimension line is to be placed: Dimension line angle <0>:. The angle may be entered explicitly or may be shown by picking two points. After the angle has been specified, the dimension form must be defined. The prompt is: First extension line origin or RETURN to select:. This gives

the choice of selecting extension line positions by picking two points or by selecting an entity to be dimensioned and letting the system find them.

- In the first case, a point is picked and the prompt: Second extension line origin: is issued. The other extension line position can then be picked.
- Otherwise, if RETURN has been entered, the user will be prompted to pick the entity to be dimensioned: Select line, arc or circle:. Appropriate extension line origins will be selected automatically; at the ends of a line or arc and at points diametrically opposed and at the specified angle on a circle.

The prompt Dimension line location (Text/Angle): appears. This expects a point, through which the dimension line must pass, to be picked.

The user will next be asked to view the default dimension text which is set to the current format: Dimension text <default>:. This can be overridden. See Figure 6.2.
If either of the options Text or Angle is selected, the operator can specify the dimension text or the angle at which it is to be drawn before selecting the point through which the dimension line is to pass.

DIM:SAve
- saves named dimension styles

Command Sequence
DIM: **Dim Styl: Save**

Command Options
The name of the style must be set in response to the prompt: ?/Name for new dimension style:. If ? is returned, a list of existing dimension styles is displayed. All currently defined styles or a subset defined by wild cards may be listed. The prompt is Dimension style(s) to list <*>:. A dimension style name can consist of up to 31 characters including hyphens, underscores and dollar signs. If the entered name is the same as a previously defined name, a replacement check prompt will be issued: That name is already in use, redefine it? <N>. Either another name can be given or the previous settings overwritten.
All the current settings of dimension variables are saved as

a named dimension style which may be used for subsequent operations.

DIM:STAtus

- lists settings of dimension variables

Command Sequence

DIM: **STATUS**

Command Options

This command has no options. The list of dimension variables is displayed on receipt of STATUS.

DIM:STYle

- changes the current text style

Command Sequence

DIM: **Dim Styl Dimstyle**

Command Options

A new text style is entered in response to the prompt New text style <default>:. The current text is shown for reference.

DIM:TEdit

- changes position or angle of dimension text

Command Sequence

DIM: Edit TEDIT

↓ Modify → Edit Dims▸ → Dimension Text▸ → Move Text

Command Options

The dimension whose text is to be modified is selected in response to the command: Select dimension:. The text may then be justified on the dimension line by selecting from the option list shown in the next prompt: Enter text location (Left/Right/Home/Angle):. If no option is selected, the text can be dragged to its desired position. If the dimension variable DIMSHO is set to 1, the text will be displayed during the drag operation.

If the option Angle is selected, a new text angle may be specified in response to the prompt: Enter text angle:. Another way to define the text angle is to pick two points. If RETURN is entered, the text angle is not changed.

DIM:TRotate

- changes the text angle for associative dimensions

Command Sequence

↓ Modify ↓ Edit Dims▸ ↓ Dimension Text> ↓ Rotate Text

Command Options

The new text angle is typed in response to the prompt: Enter text angle:. An angle may alternatively be defined by picking two points. The dimensions to be affected are selected after: Select objects:.

DIM:Undo

- cancels the effect of the previous command

Command Sequence

DIM: **Edit Undo**

Command Options

There are no options. UNDO can be repeated right back to the beginning of the current DIM command.

DIM:UPdate

- changes setting of associative dimension to current style

Command Sequence

DIM: **Edit Update**

↓ Modify → Edit Dims▸ → Update Dimension

Command Options
The appropriate dimensions are selected after the prompt Select objects: and then become updated with the current settings.

DIM:VARiables
- lists dimension variable settings

Command Sequence
DIM: **Dim Styl Variabls**

Command Options
The initial prompt is:

> Current dimension style: CURRENT
> ?/Enter dimension style name or RETURN to select dimension:.

The current style is shown for reference. Entry of ? will result in the listing of the names of named styles. The prompt: Dimension style(s) to list <*> will be issued and more than one style may be selected by using wild cards. If a named dimension style is preceded by "~", a tilde, differences between the settings of the specified style and the current setting will be displayed. The name of a style can be entered or a dimension can be selected by entering RETURN. The latter option will result in the prompt: Select dimension: and when the dimension is picked, its dimension style will be assumed for variable listing.

DIM:VErtical
- draws vertical dimensions

Command Sequence
DIM: **Vertical**
↓ **Draw** → **Dimensions▸** → **Linear▸** → **Vertical**

Command Options
The first prompt is First extension line origin or RETURN to Select: If a point is selected, then the prompt: Second extension line origin: will be issued. A point may then be

selected.

If RETURN is typed at the first prompt, the prompt Select line, arc or circle: will appear. When the entity is selected, the extension line origins will be defined automatically at its ends.

In either case, the prompt Dimension line location (Text/Angle): will be displayed. A point at which the dimension line is to pass may be picked. The Text and Angle options may be used to modify the default text and to set the dimension text to a desired angle.

The dimension will be drawn with extension lines horizontal and dimension line vertical - see Figure 6.2.

DIM1
- draws just one dimension

Command Sequence
Command: **DIM1**

Command Options
The action of this command is the same as that of DIM, except that just a single dimension is drawn, then control returns to the Command: prompt.

7 Working in 3D

3D

- creates three-dimensional objects

Command Sequence

Command: **3D**

→ **DRAW** → **next** → **3D Surfs** → **3D objects**

↓ **Draw** → **3D Surfaces**

Command Options

The objects provided are boxes, cones, dishes, domes, meshes, pyramids, sphere, tori and wedges. The prompt:

Box/Cone/DIsh/DOme/Mesh/Pyramid/Sphere/Torus /Wedge:

is displayed and a selection made from the list. After selection, the object must be sized and located.

- Box. The location of a corner of the box must be provided followed by the length, width and height. A cube may be defined by entering C after the length. The angle of rotation about its first corner is then specified.
- Cone. The base centre point is located, followed by the radii of top and bottom of the cone. If preferred, the diameter may be entered. The height is then provided. The number of segments making up the solid may also be changed from the default. This influences the smoothness of the displayed model.
- Sphere. The centre of the sphere is located, followed by its radius or diameter. The number of latitudinal and longitudinal segments making up the sphere may also be changed from the default.
- DIsh/DOme. These objects are hemispheres, a dish with its curved side down, a dome with its curved side up.
- Mesh. Four points are specified and a surface, defined by a mesh, is drawn between them. The number of segments in the M and N directions may be defined. The N direction is defined along the line joining the first and second points, the M direction along the adjacent line.
- Pyramid. The base may be defined as having three or four sides which are described by their endpoints. A three-sided pyramid has triangular sides meeting at a

single apex. A four-sided pyramid may have triangular sides meeting at an apex or may have a ridge. Another option enables frusta to be defined for both three- and four- sided pyramids.

- Torus. The torus is defined by supplying its centre point and its minor and major radii or diameters. The number of segments round the tube and circular axis may be changed from the default.
- Wedge. The corner of the wedge is specified followed by its length, width and height. Finally, its rotation about its first corner is specified.

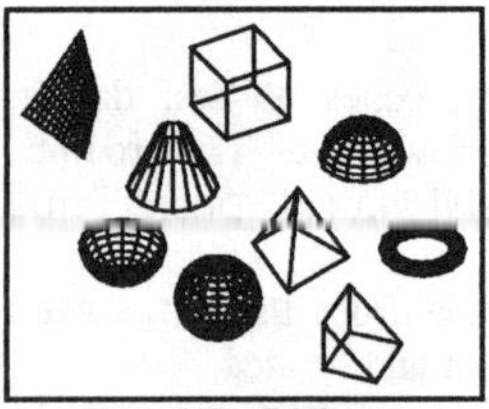

7.1a 3D Objects Unhidden

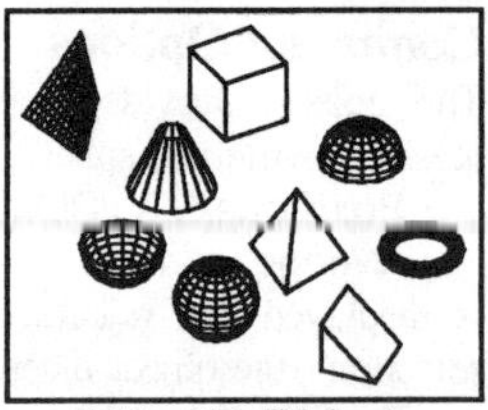

7.1b 3D Objects Hidden

3DARRAY

- creates 3D rectangular & polar arrays

Command Sequence

Command: **3DARRAY**
↓ **Construct** → **Array 3D**

Command Options

3DARRAY is the three-dimensional equivalent of the ARRAY command. Three-dimensional rectangular arrays have a number of levels in addition to the numbers of rows and columns. Three-dimensional polar arrays are similar to two-dimensional polar arrays except that the plane of the array can be tilted in space.

The objects to be replicated are selected in response to the prompt Select objects:. The next prompt is Rectangular or Polar Array (R/P)?.

- If R is selected, the numbers of rows, columns and

levels must be specified. The default on each of these is 1 which may be selected by entering RETURN in response to the prompt. Next, the distances between rows and columns, and the distance between levels, if this has been defined as greater than 1, are input.

- If P is selected, the number of repeats of the objects selected must be input. The angle subtended by the polar array is then entered, the default of 360° being selected by hitting RETURN. Next, the objects may be chosen to be rotated as they are placed in the array or to stay in the same orientation. The centre point of the array is specified and finally, a second point, which defines the axis of rotation in three dimensions, is chosen.

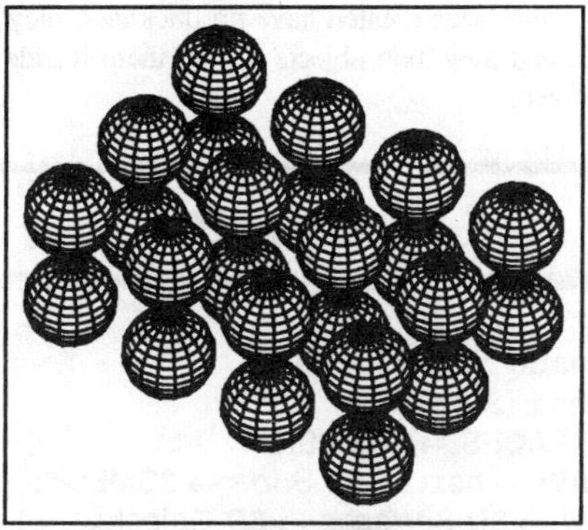

7.2 3DARRAY

3DFACE

- creates 3 & 4 sided faces

Command Sequence

Command: **3DFACE**
→ **DRAW** → **next** → **3DFACE**
→ **SURFACES** → **3DFACE**
↓ **Draw** → **3D Surfaces** → **3D Face**

Command Options

The defining points are entered cyclically around the face. Each point is defined in response to a prompt: First, Second or Third point:. At the prompt Fourth point:, either a point is defined or RETURN is entered. In the former case, a four-sided face is created; in the latter case, a three-sided face. After each group of points, another two points may be entered to create another face. The command is terminated by typing RETURN.

At each edge, modifiers may be typed or picked from the screen menu. These govern the display of the edge: I (Invisible) means the edge is invisible, S (ShowEdge) means that invisible edges are to be displayed at the next regeneration and H (HideEdge) means that hidden edges are to be made invisible at the next regeneration. The H and S options set the system variable SPLFRAME to 0 and 1 respectively.

Although the faces created have no thickness, they may be rendered and they hide objects behind them if hidden lines are removed.

3DMESH

- creates a 3D mesh of four-sided elements

Command Sequence

Command: **3DMESH**
→ **SURFACES** → **3DMESH:**
→ **DRAW** → **next** → **3D Surfs** → **3DMESH:**
↓ **Draw** → **3D Surfaces** → **3D Objects..** → **Mesh**

Command Options

The action of this command differs depending on whether it is invoked from the command line (or picked from the screen menu) or picked from the pull-down menu.

- From the command line or screen menu, the mesh sizes in each of the M and N directions are input in response to the prompts Mesh M size: and Mesh N size:. Then each of the MXN vertices is input in response to the repeated prompt Vertex (m,n): where m and n are the vertex indices.
- From the pull-down menu, only the four corners of the mesh are specified. The M and N values are input and a smooth mesh results. The N direction is defined by the line joining the first and second points.

3DPOLY
- draws a 3D polyline

Command Sequence
Command: **3DPOLY**
→ SURFACES → 3DPOLY:
→ DRAW → next → 3D Surfs → 3DPOLY:
↓ Draw → 3D Poly

Command Options
Three-dimensional polylines differ from two-dimensional polylines in that they cannot contain arc segments nor have width. They are defined point-to-point. The first prompt is From point:. When the start point has been defined, further points can be input in response to the prompt: Close/Undo/<Endpoint of line>:. The Undo option erases the last defined segment and Close draws a segment from the last point defined to the first. Although three-dimensional polylines cannot contain arcs, they may be splined using PEDIT. In this case, they are converted to approximate curves formed by short, straight lines.

DDSOLMASSP
- reports on mass properties of solids

Command Sequence
Command: **DDSOLMASSP**
→ MODEL → INQUIRY → DDSOLMASP:
↓ Model → Inquiry▸ → Mass Property

Command Options.
The command results in the prompt: Select objects:. The area, perimeter, bounding box and centroid of the regions are reported in a dialogue box after all relevant objects have been selected. The moment and product of inertia, radius of gyration, and principal directions and moments may also be reported if the XY plane of the regions lie in the same plane as the current UCS. The results may be written to a named file if the File button is clicked.

The units for the mass properties are governed by the system variable SOLMASS. Inquiries about mass properties may also be made using the SOLMASSP command which uses command line prompts.

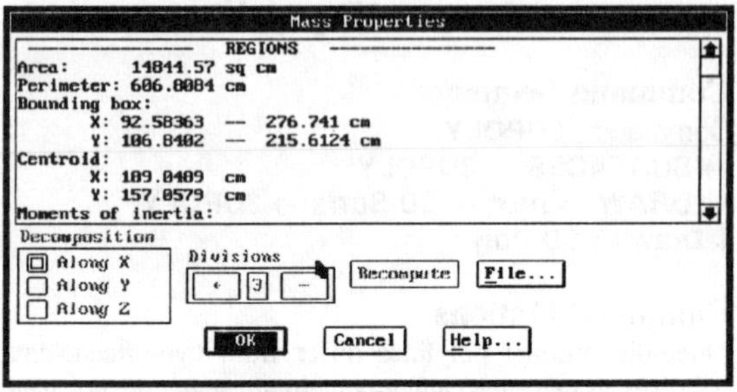

7.3 DDSOLMASSP Dialogue Box

DDSOLVAR

- sets values of solid modelling system variables

Command Sequence

Command: **DDSOLVAR**

→ **MODEL** → **UTILITY** → **SETUP** → **SOLVAR:**

↓ **Model** → **Setup** → **Variables**

Command Options

The AME System Variables dialogue box is displayed (Figure 7.4). This may be used to change the setting of selected system variables.

EDGESURF

- creates a 3D four-sided mesh

Command Sequence

Command: **EDGESURF**

→ **DRAW** → **next** → **3D Surfs** → **EDGSURF:**

↓ **Draw** → **3D Surfaces▸** → **Edge Defined Patch**

Command Options

The four bounding entities must have been defined so that they make a curved four-sided figure connected at its corners. They can be any combination of lines, arcs and

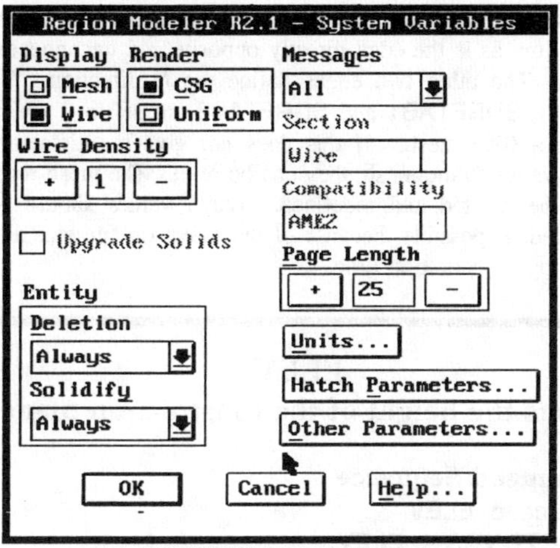

7.4 DDSOLVAR Dialogue Box

polylines. They are selected one at a time in response to the prompt: Select edge:. If there are no problems, the mesh is drawn. If the edges do not form a valid closed curved form, an error message is displayed.

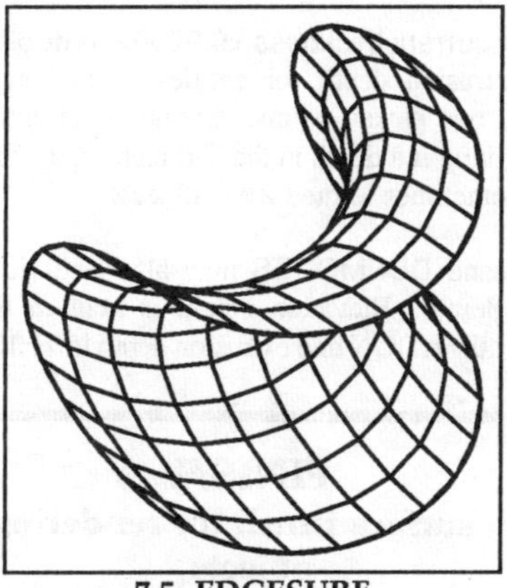

7.5 EDGESURF

The smoothness of the patch defined by the mesh is governed by the settings of the system variables SURFTAB1 and SURFTAB2. These define the number of intermediate mesh (or tabulation) points along adjacent sides of the patch. SURFTAB1 defines the number of points in the M direction, SURFTAB2 defines the number of points in the N direction. The first edge selected is in the M direction, as is the edge directly opposite and unconnected to it. The other two edges define the N direction. By default, SURFTAB1 and SURFTAB2 are set to 6 which gives a 6X6 mesh. If this does not give a satisfactory appearance to the mesh, they can be reset. The mesh must then be deleted and redefined. Large values should be avoided, if possible, because of the effect on file size and drawing regeneration time.

ELEV
- sets the height of the construction plane

Command Sequence
Command: **ELEV**
→ SETTINGS → ELEV:

Command Options
The prompt New current elevation <0.0000>: is answered by the height of the new elevation above the current UCS, a negative height being interpreted as a distance below the UCS. The height may be defined by two picked points.

Next, New current thickness <0.0000>: is displayed. This sets an extrusion depth for entities. This may also be defined by two picked points. Extruding an entity has the effect of giving it a depth in the Z-direction. Entities of this kind are sometimes termed 2½D objects.

The command DDEMODES may also be used to set an extrusion depth. Elevation height is held in the system variable ELEVATION and extrusion depth in THICKNESS.

FINISH
- sets surface finish for rendering 3D objects

Command Sequence
Command: **FINISH**
→ RENDER → FINISH
↓ Render → Finishes

Command Options

The appearance of a rendered object may be controlled by setting its illumination and its surface characteristics or finish. Five separate finish characteristics may be set using the Finish command and these settings may be named and stored for future reference.

Finish variables are:

- Colour. There are several ways of specifying a colour -RGB (Red, Green, Blue) and HLS (Hue, Luminance and Saturation) are the two available in AutoCAD.
- Ambient light. This is the light from the object's surroundings which is reflected back to the observer's eye. It is the same in all directions so that a sphere lit only by ambient light would appear as a disc. A sphere lit without ambient light would appear black where the light did not fall directly on it. In Finish, the ambient light is defined by a value from 0 to 1.
- Diffuse light. Real objects have some degree of surface roughness. The surface imperfections result in light being cast in all directions from any illuminated part of the object. A matt surface displays a lot of diffuse lighting. In Finish, the diffuse light is given a value from 0 to 1.
- Specular light. This is the degree of shininess of an object. Specular light is reflected back to the observer's eye as though from a mirror. Highlights due to specular lighting are of the same colour as the reflected light. In Finish, the specular light is given a value from 0 to 1.
- Roughness. This controls the size of highlights. A high value of roughness results in a highlight spread over a larger area than does a low value. In Finish, the roughness is given a value from 0 to 1. In order for it to have any effect, the specular value must be non-zero.

On entry to the Finish command, the Finishes dialogue box is displayed. This has several sections, some of which result in secondary dialogue boxes being displayed.

- The Finishes section shows a list of currently defined finishes, one of which is the default, named *GLOBAL*. Some may be attached to an AutoCAD Colour Index (ACI). and are shown with the ACI number appended. To operate on a particular finish, it is first highlit by being picked and then the required operation initiated by clicking on a button.
- If a new finish is to be defined, the button New... must

be clicked. This will display the New Finish dialogue box. In this box, the five finish characteristics: Colour, Ambient, Diffuse, Specular and Roughness can be set. Other options in this box are:

- Finish Name: a name is given to the defined finish.
- Use Entity Color: the finish colour is taken from the selected entities rather than being set.
- Preview Finish: the finish defined may be inspected prior to using or storing it.

- If an existing finish is to be changed, the Modify... button must be clicked after the finish has been selected in the Finishes list. This displays the Modify Finish dialogue box which is identical with the New Finish box.
- The Delete button may be used to delete a finish which has been selected in the Finishes list.
- The Import... button may be used to load a previously defined finish. This displays the Import Preset dialogue box, which shows a list of candidate finishes. A finish may be inspected before loading by clicking the Preview Finish button after selecting a finish from the list. A sphere with the selected finish will be rendered in the box.
- The Export... button is used if the highlighted finish is to be saved for importing to subsequent drawings. All preset finishes are stored in an ASCII file called NULLSURF.SP3.
- The Pick< button permits a finish to be selected from the current drawing rather than from the Finishes list. An object with the required finish is picked from the drawing and when the Finishes dialogue box is redisplayed, that finish is highlit in the Finishes list.
- Two buttons are located in an area of the Finishes dialogue box labelled Attach.
  - The Entities button allows picked entities to be assigned the finish which has been highlit.
  - The ACI button displays the Attach by AutoCAD Color Index Dialogue Box. This enables a highlit finish to be assigned to an ACI. This is a convenient way of allocating a defined finish to many objects.

HIDE

- removes hidden lines from solid objects

Command Sequence

Command: **HIDE**
→ **DISPLAY** → **HIDE**
↓ **Render** → **Hide**

Command Options

This command has no options. Hidden lines are removed from the objects in the current viewport - see Figure 7.1b. Since hidden line removal can take a long time, it is best to use the command sparingly.

ISOPLANE

- creates the isometric coordinate system

Command Sequence

Command: **ISOPLANE**

Command Options

This command results in the display of a grid with grid lines at 30, 90 and 150 degrees to the horizontal if Gridmode is set to ON by using the GRID command. These define three sets of isometric coordinates. The grid lines at 150 and 90 degrees define the left plane, The grid lines at 150 and 30 degrees define the top plane. The grid lines at 90 and 30 degrees define the right plane. The SNAP command contains a Style option Isometric which forces the cursor to snap to points on this grid.

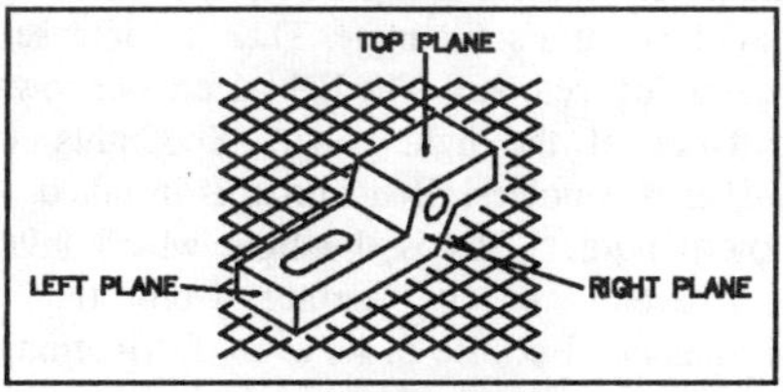

7.6 ISOPLANE

A prompt: Left/Top/Right/<Toggle>: is issued when ISOPLANE is entered. One of the isometric planes may be selected, or the next plane in cyclic sequence may be toggled. A more convenient way to toggle between the isometric planes is to use Ctrl-E. Isometric drawing is easily done using the ISOPLANE drawing aid. Lines may be drawn parallel to the isometric axes by setting ORTHO to ON (Ctrl-O is the easiest way). Isometric circles (which appear as ellipses) may be drawn by using the Isocircle: option in the Ellipse drawing command.

The system variable SNAPISOPAIR is set by toggling to one of the three planes. It can have values: 0 = left plane, 1 = top plane and 2 = right plane.

LIGHT

- creates and locates lights for rendering

Command Sequence

Command: **LIGHT**
→ **RENDER** → **LIGHT**
↓ **Render** → **Lights**

Command Options

There are four kinds of light that can be specified using the LIGHT command.

- Point lights. These emit light equally in all directions like light bulbs. The intensity of light falling on an object decreases the further the object is away from the light.
- Distant lights. These, like the sun, emit light in a set direction.
- Spotlights. These emit light in a cone. The light falls on an object at a solid angle. There is intense light at the centre of the cone. The light decreases towards the boundaries of the light cone. Spotlights are only available if AutoDesk Renderman is installed.
- Ambient light. This is the light which falls on an object evenly on its surface from the object's environment. Because of its even distribution, it does not cast a shadow.

The command LIGHT produces the Lights dialogue box. This contains a lights name list and three groups of buttons apart from the usual OK, Cancel and Help... buttons.

- The lights name list shows the lights currently available.
- The New... button when clicked produces a New dialogue box. From this can be picked, using a radio button, one type of light from Point Light, Distant Light or Spotlight. The last is available only if AutoDesk Renderman is installed. A dialogue for the light type chosen will be displayed. This can be used to give a light a name (eight or less characters). Light Intensity can be set using a slider bar, its current value being shown in a small box in which an explicit value may be typed if preferred. Distant lights may have a maximum intensity value of 1 since they are assumed to be so far away from the an object's locality that there is no intensity fade. The Modify< button initiates the placing of a light. Show... displays the light in its X, Y and Z location. Modify Light Color... and Depth Map Size are available only if AutoDesk Renderman is installed; otherwise they are greyed out.
- The Modify... button produces a Modify Light dialogue box. This is similar to the New Light dialogue box.
- The Delete button may be used to delete a light from the lights name list.
- Pick< results in the dialogue box temporarily disappearing so that a light may be picked from the screen and modified or deleted.
- Ambient Light intensity may be set directly on the Lights dialogue box by using the slider provided.
- Point Light fall-off can be set by using one of three radio buttons on the Lights dialogue box. None results in no fall-off taking place. Inverse Linear fall-off causes a light's intensity to diminish inversely with the distance from it. Inverse Square fall-off causes a light's intensity to diminish inversely as the square of the distance from the light source.

MIRROR3D*

- mirrors entities about a plane

Command Sequence

Command: **MIRROR3D**

→ EDIT → next → MIRROR: → 3D MIRROR

↓ Construct → Mirror 3D

Command Options

This command is the three-dimensional equivalent of the two-dimensional MIRROR and its action is the same except that entities are mirrored about a plane rather than a line and there are more ways to define a plane than there are to define a line.

The first prompt is: Select objects:. The entities to be mirrored are selected by picking, windowing or any of the other selection methods. When all the objects have been selected (signalled by entering RETURN to the prompt), the mirror plane must be defined.

Plane by Entity/Last/Zaxis/View/XY/YZ/<3points>: is the option list for plane selection.

- Entity requires the mirror plane to be specified by selecting a two-dimensional entity whose construction plane will be taken as the mirror plane. The system asks for a circle, arc or 2D polyline segment to be picked.
- Last indicates that the last mirror plane should be used again. If there is no previous plane, an error message results.
- Zaxis requires the mirror plane to be specified by selecting a point on the current construction plane and a point on its Z-axis. The mirror plane is then parallel with the construction plane and passes through the Z-point.
- View results in the mirror plane being defined as parallel with the viewing plane and passing through a point, the coordinates of which are input.
- XY results in the mirror plane being defined as parallel with the XY plane and passing through a point, the coordinates of which are input.
- YZ results in the mirror plane being defined as parallel with the YZ plane and passing through a point, the coordinates of which are input.
- ZX results in the mirror plane being defined as parallel with the ZX plane and passing through a point, the coordinates of which are input.
- The default option is <3points> which requires the mirror plane to be specified by entering three non-collinear points.

The final prompt is: Delete old objects? <N>: which determines whether the original entities are left in position.

PEDIT(3D)

- edits 3D polylines and polygon meshes

Command Sequence

Command: **PEDIT**

→ **EDIT** → **next** → **PEDIT:**

↓ **Modify** → **PolyEdit**

Command Options

On entry to PEDIT, the entity to be edited is selected. If this is a 3D polyline or a mesh, a set of options are available which are different from those presented when a 2D polyline is picked.

The first prompt, if a 3D polyline is selected, is:
Close/Edit vertex/Spline curve/Decurve/Undo/eXit <X>:
This list of options is shorter than those for 2D polylines since a 3D polyline has no width and 3D spline curves are made from straight line segments. The options listed work in the same way as those for a 2D polyline.

If a 3D mesh is selected, the first prompt is:
Edit vertex/Smooth surface/Desmooth/Mclose/Nclose/ Undo/eXit/ <X>:

- Edit vertex displays a second prompt Vertex(m,n). Next/Previous/Left/RIght/Up/Down/Move/REgen/eXit <X>:. This enables individual vertices of the mesh to be moved around in three-dimensional space. This is done by driving a vertex marker, showing the current mesh node, around the mesh using the directions Left, RIght, Up and Down until the marker is at the desired position. The vertex may then be moved to a new position in 3-space. Regen restores the display of an edited polyline.
- Smooth surface has different actions depending on the value of the system variable SURFTYPE. If SURFTYPE is 5, the mesh is smoothed by quadratic B-spline smoothing. If it is 6, the mesh is smoothed by cubic B-spline smoothing. If it is 8, it is smoothed by Bézier patch smoothing. The system variables SURFU and SURFV determine the number of control points in the M and N directions respectively.
- Desmooth restores the original mesh. The mesh now passes through the mesh points rather than regarding

them as control points.

- Mclose closes the mesh in the M direction.
- Nclose closes the mesh in the N direction.
- Undo cancels the previous mesh editing operation.
- eXit terminates the command.

PFACE

- creates a polygon mesh bounded by points

Command Sequence

Command: **PFACE**

→ **DRAW** → **next** →**3D Surfs** → **PFACE:**

Command Options

A series of points is specified in response to the repeated prompt Vertex n:. Here, n is the vertex number; it is incremented as each point is supplied. The completion of point definition is signalled by typing RETURN.

Next, the edges are defined by entering the vertex numbers which will make up the edges of the face. The prompt is Face m, Vertex n: where m is the face number and n is the vertex number . The edge number remains the same until all the vertex numbers are input - signalled by RETURN - then it is incremented.

After the last face, another RETURN terminates the command.

RENDER

- renders an image

Command Sequence

Command: **RENDER**

→ **RENDER** → **RENDER:**

↓ **Render** → **Render**

Command Options

There are no prompts issued and the rendered image is produced directly. The lighting has the settings previously defined by using the command LIGHT. The finish on objects is according to settings produced by the command FINISH. Other settings, such as whether full or quick rendering is to be carried out, are provided by RPREF.

RENDSCR

- displays the last rendered image

Command Sequence

Command: **RENDSCR**

Command Options

There are no prompts issued by this command. The last rendered image is displayed. The normal drawing editor may be returned to by hitting any key.

REPLAY

- displays an imported raster image

Command Sequence

Command: **REPLAY**
→ **RENDER** → **REPLAY**
↓ **Render** → **Files** → **Replay Image**

Command Options

The types of file that can be displayed using the REPLAY command are:

- GIF: CompuServe Graphics Interchange Format
- RND: AutoShade format
- TGA: Targa format.
- TIFF: Tagged Input File Format.

The Replay File dialogue box is displayed. A file is selected using the file list and possibly wild card settings.

When this has been done, the Image Specification dialogue box is displayed. In this box, a screen offset for the portion of the display allocated for the bit-mapped image may be set. Inside this, the image may be positioned using offset and size values in pixels.

REVSURF
- creates a surface of revolution

Command Sequence
Command: **REVSURF**
→ DRAW → next → 3D Surfs → REVSURF:
↓ Draw → 3D Surfaces▸ → Surface of Revolution

Command Options
The surface of revolution is created by rotating a profile around an axis of revolution. The profile may be a line, arc,circle or polyline and is picked in response to the prompt: Select path curve:

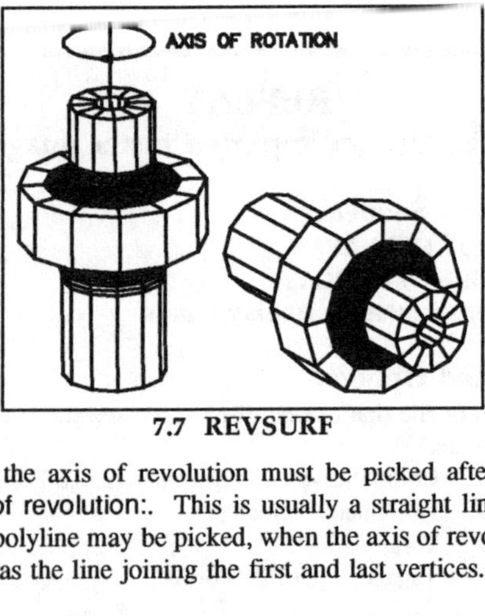

7.7 REVSURF

Next, the axis of revolution must be picked after Select axis of revolution:. This is usually a straight line but an open polyline may be picked, when the axis of revolution is taken as the line joining the first and last vertices.

The start angle must be specified after Start angle <0>:. Then the prompt Included angle (+=ccw, -=cw) <Full circle>: requires the swept angle to be defined. The axis of rotation determines the M direction of the surface formed and the N direction is in the sweep direction.

The point picked on the axis of rotation determines the angle through which the profile will be rotated. The positive direction of rotation around an axis is clockwise looking along the axis toward the origin.

The resolution of the mesh is controlled by the system variables SURFTAB1, the number of mesh segments in the M direction, and SURFTAB2, the number of segments in the N direction.

ROTATE3D*

- rotates an object about a 3D axis

Command Sequence

Command: **ROTATE3D**
→ **EDIT** → **next** → **ROTATE:** → **3D ROTATE**
↓ **Modify** → **Rotate 3D**

Command Options

The objects for rotation are picked after Select objects:. Next, the rotation axis must be defined after the prompt: Axis by Entity/Last/View/Xaxis/Yaxis/Zaxis/<2points>:. The prompts present different methods of defining the axis.

- Entity defines the axis by reference to an existing entity. The prompt Pick a line, circle, arc or 2D-polyline segment appears. If the circle or arc options are chosen, the axis of rotation is through the centre of the circle or arc and at right angles to its plane.
- Last selects the previous rotation axis, if possible.
- View defines the rotation plane as the plane of the current view. The axis of rotation passes through a point picked in response to the prompt: Point on view direction axis <0,0,0>:
- Xaxis, Yaxis and Zaxis define the direction of the axis. The axis passes through a point which is picked after a prompt of the form: Point on X axis <0,0,0>:.
- 2point defines the axis of rotation as passing through two points picked in response to the prompts: 1st point on axis: and 2nd point on axis:.

RPREF

- set rendering preferences

Command Sequence

Command: RPREF
→ **RENDER** → **RPREF**
↓ **Render** → **Preferences**

Command Options

The Rendering Preferences dialogue box is displayed. This contains eight groups of options in addition to the usual OK, Cancel and Help....

- Rendering Type group contains options for Full and Quick Render, and ACAD RenderMan, the last being active only if RenderMan has been installed. Full Render is used for final images, Quick Render to preview quickly how the final image will look. If Full Render is selected, the Full Rendering dialogue box will appear. This supports options for rendering only in black and white, for rendering the separate components of red, green and blue and several other options governing the quality of images.
- Rendering Options group contains buttons for Smooth Shading, Merge, Apply Finishes and one for More Options.... Smooth Shading results in a gradual transition between the shading on adjacent facets. Merge permits several images to be merged in the frame-buffer, If Apply Finishes is ON, the defined finishes of rendered objects will be in force. If it is OFF, the *GLOBAL* finish will be applied. More Options turns on the Full or Quick Render Options dialogue box.
- Select Query is a drop-down list permitting all or selected objects to be rendered.
- Destination group contains two options permitting rendered images to be sent to the display or to a hardcopy device.
- Color Map Usage group forces the way AutoCAD uses colours on the rendering for 256 colour displays. The three options are: Best Map/No Fold, Best Map/Fold and Fixed ACAD Map. Best Map/No Fold results in AutoCAD using only the 240 non-reserved colours. Best Map/Fold uses all 256 colours. Fixed ACAD Map forces AutoCAD to used the fixed settings which for most applications gives the worst rendering.
- Settings group contains two options. RMan prompting, if AutoShade has been installed, permits more sophisticated rendering to be performed. The Icon Scale option determines the scale for light and finish icons.
- Information... may be used to display a copyright notice and details of the display configuration.
- Reconfigure> executes the RCONFIG command enabling the configuration for rendering to be changed.

RULESURF

- creates a mesh between two entities

Command Sequence

Command: **RULESURF**
→ **DRAW** → **next** → **3D Surfs** → **RULESURF:**
↓ **Draw** → **3D Surfaces▸** → **Ruled Surface**

Command Options.

The two entities, which may be points, lines, arcs or polylines, are selected in response to the prompts Select first defining curve: and Select second defining curve:. The position at which an entity is picked is important since the nearest end to the pick point becomes the start point of the mesh. One of the entities may be a point.

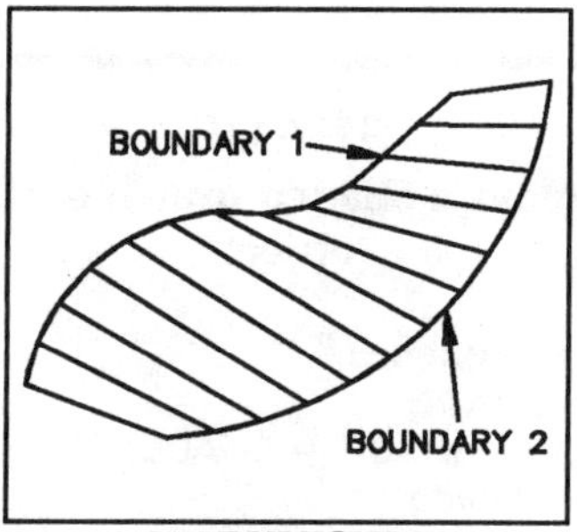

7.8 RULESURF

If one of the entities is a circle or closed polyline, the other entity cannot be closed. It is legal for one entity to be a point. The number of segments along the entities is governed by the system variable SURFTAB1.

SCENE*

- creates, loads & changes scenes

Command Sequence

Command: **SCENE**
→ **RENDER** → **SCENE**
↓ **Render** → **Scenes**

Command Options

A scene is a view together with its lighting. The Scenes dialogue box, displayed on issue of the command contains a list of currently defined scenes. A scene in the list can be highlit. One of three buttons may then be clicked - New..., Modify... and Delete.... Clicking the last button results in the highlit scene being deleted. The other two cause dialogue boxes to be displayed.

- The New Scene dialogue box has an edit box for specifying or changing the name of a scene. There is a views list which shows all the views in the current drawing. To change the view, it should be picked in the list. There is also a list of lights. These can be added to the current scene. There is a name *ALL*, which adds all the lights to the scene.
- The Modify Scene dialogue box has the same layout as the New Scene dialogue box but its purpose is to edit existing views rather than create new ones.

SHADE

- displays a shaded drawing of a 3D object

Command Sequence

Command: **SHADE**
→ **DISPLAY** → **SHADE** → **SHADE:**
↓ **Render** → **Shade**

Command Options

SHADE produces a shaded image of three-dimensional objects by filling each face with a solid colour. The image may be saved using MSLIDE.

The system variable SHADEDGE governs the colour in which edges of the model are drawn. The system variable SHADEDIF governs the ratio between diffuse and ambient light on the model. The lighting is fixed in a position normal to the screen.

The shading is removed at the next regeneration of the drawing.

SOLAREA

- returns the surface area of solid objects

Command Sequence

Command: **SOLAREA**

→ **MODEL** → **INQUIRY** → **SOLAREA:**

↓ **Model** → **INQUIRY>** → **Area Calc**

Command Options

The objects are selected in response to the prompt: Select objects:. The total surface area of the objects picked is then reported in the units set in the system variable SOLAREAU.

SOLCHP

- changes properties of a solid primitive

Command Sequence

Command: **SOLCHP**

→ **MODEL** → **MODIFY** → **SOLCHP:**

↓ **Model** → **Modify** → **Change Prim.**

Command Options

The first prompt is Select a solid or region:. This is selected by picking. Since the command operates only on primitives, if a composite region is selected, the system prompts: Select primitive: and the primitive is picked on the solid object. If the primitive highlighted is not the one required, Next is chosen in the prompt which follows. Another primitive is highlighted and the procedure may be repeated if necessary. The next prompt is:

Color/Delete/Evaluate/Instance/Move/Next/Pick/
Replace/Size/eXit <N>:.

- Color may be used to change the entity's colour. The new colour is specified by name or by standard number.
- Delete may be used to erase the selected entity. If the entity was part of a composite solid, this option may be used to separate it out from the solid.
- Evaluate causes a regeneration of the composite region so that the results of changes may be observed.
- Instance creates a new instance or separate copy of the entity. This overlays the existing primitive.

- Move translates the primitive. A base point and the point of displacement are required.
- Next is used to cycle through the primitives in a composite region.
- Pick permits a primitive to be selected by picking.
- Replace changes the selected primitive to another entity. A Select solid to replace primitive... prompt is displayed, after which the new solid may be selected. If the original solid is part of a composite region, the new solid takes its place although it is not moved in any way. The original primitive may be retained though detached from the composite region.
- Size changes any dimensions of the primitive. Current dimensions in the X-, Y- and Z-directions are displayed.
- Exit leaves the SOLCHP command.

SOLDISP*

- changes a solid or composite region to a mesh

Command Sequence

Command: **SOLDISP**

Command Options

This command is usually used before rendering to provide a high quality image. An option is chosen from the list in the prompt: Mesh/<Wire>: and the objects to be changed picked after the prompt: Select objects:.

The system variable SOLDISPLAY controls the mode of representation of entities. The AME (Advanced Modelling Extension) automatically changes the mode of all its entities to Mesh before rendering is carried out.

SOLFEAT

- creates a 2D block from an edge or face of a solid object

Command Sequence

Command: **SOLFEAT**

→ **MODEL** → **DISPLAY** → **SOLFEAT:**

↓ **Model** → **Display** → **Copy Feature**

Command Options

SOLFEAT (SOLid FEATure) is used to create 2D views from 3D objects. On entry to the command, the first prompt is Edge/<Face>:.

- If the Edge option is chosen, the prompt All/<Select>: appears. The All option results in blocks being made from each edge in the selected object. The Select option requires edges to be picked one by one. If a mesh is selected, rather than a wire frame, the entity is changed to a wire frame representation before edge selection is made. In this case, the prompt: PMESH region. Change it to WIREFRAME for feature selection? <Y>:. If Y is returned, the edges may be picked from the resulting wire frame. If the answer is N, another entity must be picked or the command terminated.
- If the Face option is chosen, the prompt All/<Select>: appears. The All option results in blocks being made from each face in the selected object. The Select option requires faces to be picked one by one. If a mesh is selected, the action is similar to that for the Edge option.

Blocks created are not moved but are created on the current layer in the same position as the features from which they are derived.

SOLIDIFY

- changes 2D entities into solid regions

Command Sequence

Command: **SOLIDIFY**
→ **MODEL** → **SOLIDIFY**
↓ **Model** → **Solidify**

Command Options

Objects are chosen in response to the prompt: Select objects:. These are then converted into solid regions. Valid objects are: circles, ellipses, doughnuts, polylines, polygons, traces and 2D solid entities.

Before solidifying, open polylines are closed. If they have width, the solid region is bounded by their centrelines.

If the system variable SOLDELENT is set, the selected objects will be deleted after solidification. If system variable SOLSOLIDIFY is set, other solid commands will solidify entities when they are invoked.

SOLINT

- forms the intersection of two or more regions

Command Sequence

Command: **SOLINT**
→ **MODEL** → **SOLINT:**
↓ **Model** → **Intersect**

Command Options

The objects are selected after the prompt Select objects:. When selection is terminated by entering RETURN, a composite region is created from the Boolean intersection of the selected objects. If an object is not a region, it is discarded unless the system variable SOLSOLIDIFY is set.

SOLLIST

- reports on the properties of a face, edge or CSG tree of a region

Command Sequence

Command: **SOLLIST**
→ **MODEL** → **INQUIRY** → **SOLLIST:**
↓ **Model** → **Inquiry▸** → **List Objects**

Command Options

The prompt Edge/Face/Tree/<Object>: is issued. The objects are selected and a report is displayed. The information shown depends on the type of object selected.

The system variable SOLPAGELEN controls the number of lines on each page of the report.

SOLMASSP

- reports the mass properties of a solid region

Command Sequence

Command: **SOLMASSP**
→ **MODEL** → **INQUIRY** → **SOLMASP:**
↓ **Model** → **Inquiry▸** → **Mass Property**

Command Options

The command results in the prompt: Select objects:. The area, perimeter, bounding box and centroid of the regions are reported after all relevant objects have been selected. The moment and product of inertia, radius of gyration, and principal directions and moments may also be reported if the X-Y plane of the regions lie in the same plane as the current UCS. The results may be written to a named file using a File dialogue box if the system variable FILEDIA is set to 1, or entered on the command line in response to prompts otherwise.

The units for the mass properties is governed by the system variable SOLMASS. Inquiries about mass properties may also be made with the DDSOLMASSP command which uses a dialogue box.

SOLMESH

- converts solids from wireframes to meshes

Command Sequence

Command: **SOLMESH**
→ **MODEL** → **DISPLAY** → **SOLMESH:**
↓ **Model** → **Display** → **Mesh**

Command Options

Select objects: is displayed and the objects for conversion are picked.

The system variable SOLWDENS controls the density of meshes. The system variable SOLDISPLAY is set by the SOLMESH command.

SOLMOVE

- translates and rotates solid objects

Command Sequence

Command: **SOLMOVE**

→ **MODEL** → **MODIFY** → **SOLMOVE:**

↓ **Model** → **Modify** → **Move Object**

Command Options

For this command, a Motion Coordinate System (MCS) is set up. This is the datum for all movement initiated by the command and has its own icon. It can be reset to various positions within the command but by default its origin is the origin of the X, Y and Z axes and it is oriented to the current UCS.

The objects to be moved are selected in response to the prompt Select objects:. The operations to be carried out on the objects are defined by one or more motion description codes. A list of the possible codes may be displayed by selecting ? from the option list ?/<Motion description>:. This prompt is displayed repeatedly until the desired motion has been obtained at which point entry of RETURN terminates the command.

The codes consist of a letter defining the operation followed by a modifier selected from a list. The list is shown in square brackets.

- A[efuw]: aligns objects with a coordinate system: e = edge, f = face, u = UCS, w = WCS.
- R[xyz]: rotates objects about an axis chosen from [xyz]. A rotation angle follows the codes.
- T[xyz]: moves objects along an axis chosen from [xyz]. A translation distance follows the codes.
- E: sets MCS to align with a selected edge.
- F: sets MCS to align with a selected face.
- U: sets MCS to the UCS.
- W: sets MCS to the WCS.
- O: restores objects to their original conditions.

SOLPURGE

- erases database information about solid objects

Command Sequence

Command: **SOLPURGE**
→ **MODELS → UTILITY → SOLPURG:**
↓ **Model → UTILITY▸ → Purge Objects**

Command Options

The object of holding information about solid objects is to reduce calculation time when they are processed. If storage is short, it might be considered desirable to forfeit speed of processing in the interests of storage conservation. In the SOLPURGE command, it is possible to elect to purge those objects which have a stable definition, leaving intact extraneous information about objects which may change often.

Memory/2Dtree/Bfile/Pmesh/<Erased>: is displayed.

- Memory has two possible options: All and Select. All purges information from all defined solid objects; Select provides the facility for selective purging.
- 2Dtree (Release 12 only) simplifies the structure of a region.
- Bfile purges boundary files from solids.
- Pmesh changes the representation from mesh to wire frame.

SOLSEP

- dissects composite solids into their components

Command Sequence

Command: **SOLSEP**
→ **MODEL → MODIFY → SOLSEP:**
↓ **Model → Modify → Separate**

Command Options

Solid objects may have been combined into composite regions by the Boolean operations SOLINT, SOLUNION and SOLSUB. The command SOLSEP reverses these operations.

The composite objects are selected after the Select Objects: prompt. They are then reduced to primitives.

SOLSUB
- Boolean subtracts solid objects

Command Sequence
Command: **SOLSUB**
→ **MODEL** → **SOLSUB:**
↓ **Model** → **Subtract**

Command Options
One set of solid objects is Boolean subtracted from another set of solid objects to form a new composite region. The first set of objects is picked after the prompt: Source Objects... Select objects:.

The second set of objects is picked after the prompt: Objects to select from them ... Select objects:. The composite object is created if all is well. If not, error messages will be displayed.

SOLUCS
- aligns the UCS with a face or edge of a solid object

Command Sequence
Command: **SOLUCS**
→ **MODEL** → **UTILITY** → **SOLUCS:**
↓ **Model** → **UTILITY▸** → **SoLUCS**

Command Options
First, the type of alignment is selected in response to the prompt Edge/<Face>:. Either Pick an edge... or Pick a face... will result depending on the feature selected.

Then, either the face or edge with which the UCS is to be aligned is selected. A face is picked by selecting one of its edges. The system highlights the face selected. The prompt: <OK>/Next: appears.

If the highlighted face is the selection intended, RETURN leaves the command; if the face is not the one intended, Next is chosen and an adjacent face is highlighted.

SOLUNION

- creates the Boolean union of two or more solids

Command Sequence

Command: **SOLUNION**
→ **MODEL** → **SOLUNION:**
↓ **Model** → **Union**

Command Options

After Select objects:, the solid objects are picked and their union created.

The union is a single object. There is no reason why this should be in one piece; if the objects are disjoint before the union is carried out, the result will appear disjoint also. It will, however, be one solid object.

SOLVAR

- lists and sets solid modelling system variables

Command Sequence

Command: **SOLVAR**
→ **MODEL** → **UTILITY** → **SETUP** → **SOLVAR:**
↓ **Model** → **Setup** → **Variables**

Command Options

The prompt Variable name or ?: is displayed. If ? is chosen, a list of system variables is displayed. If the name of a system variable is entered, its value can be changed.

This command is the command line counterpart of DDSOLVAR, which uses a dialogue box.

SOLWIRE

- converts solids from mesh to wireframe representation

Command Sequence

Command: **SOLWIRE**
→ **MODEL** → **DISPLAY** → **SOLWIRE**
↓ **Model** → **Display** → **Wireframe**

Command Options

SOLWIRE is used mainly when it is needed to edit an object using object snaps since this cannot be done using the mesh representation. The solid objects whose representations are to be converted are selected after the prompt Select objects..

The wireframe representation may be converted back to a mesh by using the SOLMESH command. This must be done if the object is to be rendered, since rendering only works on meshes.

When an object is converted into a wireframe representation, its mesh representation is not lost. It is placed on a layer called AME_FRZ automatically and the layer frozen.

STATS

- provides information about the last rendering

Command Sequence

Command: **STATS**
→ **RENDER** → **STATS**
↓ **Render** → **Statistics**

Command Options

A selection of statistics about the last rendering is displayed. This can be saved to a file in ASCII form, a check box and edit box being provided being displayed for that purpose. Information provided is:

- Scene name, if any
- Rendering type: full or quick

- Total faces
- Total triangles
- Cyclic overlaps corrected
- Triangles chopped
- Original extents
- Projected extents

TABSURF

- creates a tabulated surface

Command Sequence

Command: **TABSURF**

→ **DRAW** → **next** → **3D Surfs** → **TABSURF:**

→ **SURFACES** → **TABSURF:**

↓ **Draw** → **3D Surfaces** → **Tabulated Cylinder**

Command Options

A tabulated surface is the surface created by sweeping a curve along a straight line (or direction vector). At the prompt Select curve:, a line, arc, circle or polyline is selected. The line along which the curve is to be swept is selected after Select direction vector:.

The surface produced is a 2xN mesh, the N direction being along the swept curve. The path curve and the direction vector are not part of the tabulated surface; they are still in existence after the surface has been created. The system variable SURFTAB1 holds the number of mesh segments along the swept curve and can be used to control its smoothness.

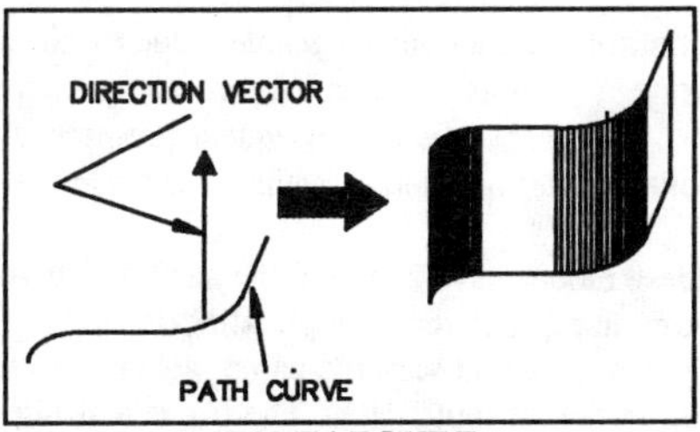

7.9 TABSURF

8 Blocks & Attributes

ATTDEF
- attaches attributes to a block definition

Command Sequence

Command: **ATTDEF**
→ **DRAW** → **ATTDEF**

Command Options

An attribute is a piece of text - descriptive or numbers - added to a block. Attributes are useful for such applications as preparing bills of materials.

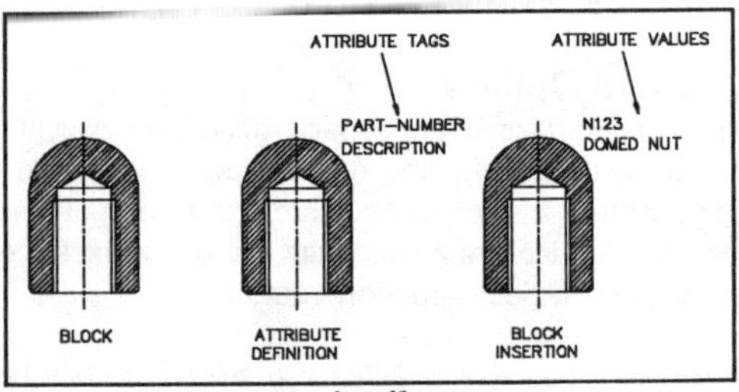

8.1 Attributes

The attribute characteristics are set using a selection from the options in the prompt Enter (ICVP) to change, RETURN when done:. The options are:

- Invisible: controls whether the attribute is shown when the block is drawn. It sets the system variable ATTMODE.
- Constant: sets an unchangeable value for the attribute.
- Verify: results in verification being required for responses to subsequent prompts.
- Preset: defines default values for attributes.

When these modes have been set, the attribute tag name will be required in reply to the prompt: Attribute tag:. This may be thought of as a text variable name attached to the block and holding the attribute data. The tag is a string of up to 31 characters. It cannot include spaces.

When a block with an attribute is inserted into a drawing, the user will be asked for the attribute's value. The prompt for this purpose will be typed in response to Attribute prompt:. If the user does not type an attribute value, the value may be set to a default. This may be entered at the prompt: Default attribute value:.

ATTDEF uses the current text style. The Height, Insertion Point, Justification and Rotation of the text may be changed. Attributes may also be set up using the Release 12 DDATTDEF command.

ATTDISP
- sets attribute visibility

Command Sequence
Command: **ATTDISP**
→ **DISPLAY** → **ATTDISP:**
'ATTDEF (Release 12 only).

Command Options
The visibility of an attribute may be set up, when the attribute is defined, using ATTDEF or DDATTDEF. ATTDISP is used to override the defined mode. The prompt: Normal/ON/OFF <Normal>: is issued.

- Normal: uses the defined mode.
- ON: turns on visiblity. Attributes are shown.
- OFF: turns off visibility. Attributes are hidden.

ATTEDIT
- edits attributes

Command Sequence
Command: **ATTEDIT**
→ **EDIT** → **ATTEDIT**

Command Options
The user is given the opportunity of editing all attributes of a block or editing them one at a time. The prompt is Edit attributes one at a time? <Y>:. Next, the block containing the attributes is defined in response to the prompt: Block name specification <*>:. The tags which are to be edited are selected after: Attribute tag specification <*>:. Attributes with specific values may be edited globally. The

prompt is: Attribute value specification <*>:.

If attributes are to be edited individually, they are specified after: Select attributes:. Invisible attributes must first be made visible using the ATTDISP command.

The editing is carried out choosing options selected from Value/Position/Height/Angle/Style/Layer/Color/Next <N>:

- Value: selected if attribute value is to be changed.
- Position: permits a new attribute position to be picked.
- Height: used for changing the value's text height.
- Angle: used for changing the value's text angle.
- Style: used for changing the text style.
- Layer: used to assign a new layer for the attribute.
- Color: used to change the colour of attribute text.
- Next: starts editing of the next attribute.

RETURN exits from the ATTEDIT command. Attributes may also be edited using the Release 12 DDATTE command.

ATTEXT
- extracts attributes and stores them

Command Sequence
Command: **ATTEXT**
→ **UTILITY** → **ATTEXT:**

Command Options
In order to store attribute information to be transferred to an external program using ATTEXT (or its dialogue box counterpart DDATTEXT), it is necessary to have first set up a template for the file. This may be done outside AutoCAD using a text editor, or inside the drawing editor by using the SHELL command. If the template file is small, the latter may be done conveniently by using the MS-DOS COPY CON <File-name> command.

The template file contains definitions, one line for each attribute. The first element in each line is the tag name of the attribute concerned. This is followed (after a space) by a value format code which determines how the attribute value is to be stored. The code has the following elements in order:

- Either C or N. C denotes that the attribute value is character information. N denotes that the value is numeric.
- A three digit number which defines the field width of the value to be stored. This should be in the range 001 to 999. Leading zeros should be added to make up the three digits.
- Finally, a three digit number which defines the number of decimal places if the attribute is numeric. If the value is a character string, this should be set to 000. Again, leading zeros should be added if necessary.

If the SHELL command has been used to exit temporarily to the operating system, a return to the drawing editor may be made by typing EXIT at the operating system prompt.

On using the command ATTEXT, assuming a template file has previously been set up, the first prompt is: CDF, SDF or DXF Attribute extract (or Entities)? <C>:. This is needed to define the format of the output file,which is done by selecting from:

- CDF: which means Comma Delimited Format, a format readable by many database systems as well as by Basic programs.
- SDF: which means Space Delimited Format, which is useful if the file is to be input to a wordprocessor. Database systems can usually cope with this format.
- DXF: or Drawing Interchange Format which permits the attribute information from the whole drawing to be stored. No template is needed in this format.

The Entities option enables attribute information to be abstracted from specified entities. Attributes may also be extracted using the Release 12 DDATTEXT command.

BASE
- sets an insertion point on the drawing

Command Sequence

Command: **BASE**

→ **BLOCKS** → **BASE:**

'BASE (Release 12 only).

Command Options

A base point is the reference point on the drawing for

insertion. The command returns the prompt: Base point: after which a base point should be picked or defined by typing in its coordinates. If only two coordinates are typed, it is assumed that the Z coordinate lies on the current elevation.

The command sets the system variable INSBASE.

BLOCK
- creates a block

Command Sequence

Command: **BLOCK**
→ **BLOCKS** → **BLOCK:**

Command Options

A block is a collection of drawing objects which may be treated as an entity. The block must be named, its component objects defined and its insertion point specified.

In response to the prompt Block name (or ?):, a name of not more than 31 characters (no spaces) is typed. If the ? option is selected, the names of blocks already defined can be listed, possibly using wild cards.

Next, an insertion base point must be defined. This governs the position at which the block will be placed when it is called up. After the prompt Insertion base point:, the desired point may be defined using a pick or by entering coordinates.

Select objects: is displayed after the insertion point has been defined. Objects to be included in the block are selected. After the block has been defined, the entities making it up are erased. They may be brought back again by using the command OOPS. The objects now have no separate existence. They may be restored to entities by using the EXPLODE command. Blocks defined by the BLOCK command can only be used on the current drawing. If they are to be used on other drawings, they must be created by the WBLOCK command.

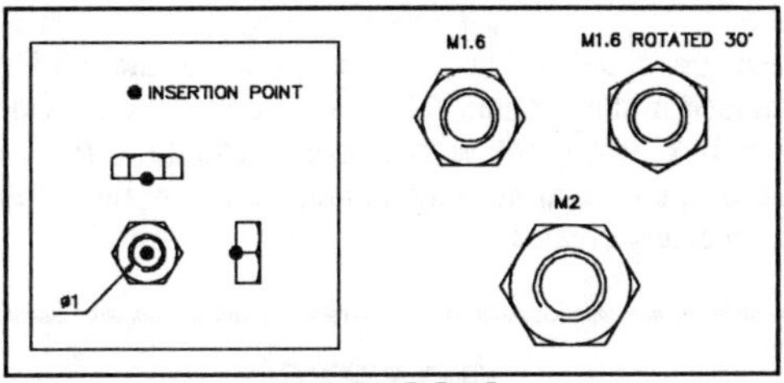

8.2 BLOCKS

DDATTDEF*

- creates block attributes

Command Sequence

→ DRAW → ATTDEF: → AttDef Dialogue
↓ DRAW → TEXT → ATTRIBUTES → DEFINE...

Command Options

Apart from the standard dialogue box OK, Cancel and Help... buttons, there are four sections on the dialogue box which is displayed. These are:

- Mode check boxes for making the attribute invisible, constant, verifiable or preset.
- Attribute edit boxes for the attribute's tag name, prompt text and default.
- An Insertion Point box giving a choice between picking the point or providing its coordinates.
- Text options for setting the text height, justification, rotation and style.

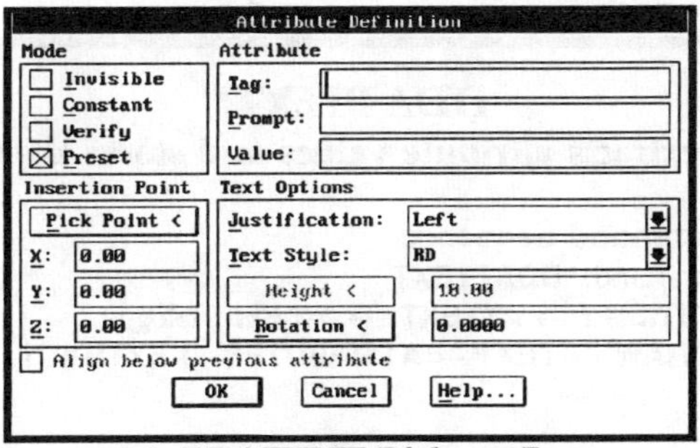

8.3 DDATTDEF Dialogue Box

These are detailed in the description of the ATTDEF command in this section. The dialogue box also provides a check box Align below previous attribute. If this is clicked, the current attribute is aligned below the attribute most recently created.

DDATTE
- edits attribute text

Command Sequence
Command: **DDATTE**
→ **EDIT** → **DDATTE:**

Command Options
A block is selected in response to the prompt Select block:. A dialogue box displaying a group of the attribute values for that block appears. Each value may be edited. The block has two buttons: Previous and Next. These can be used to move up and down through the block's attribute values.

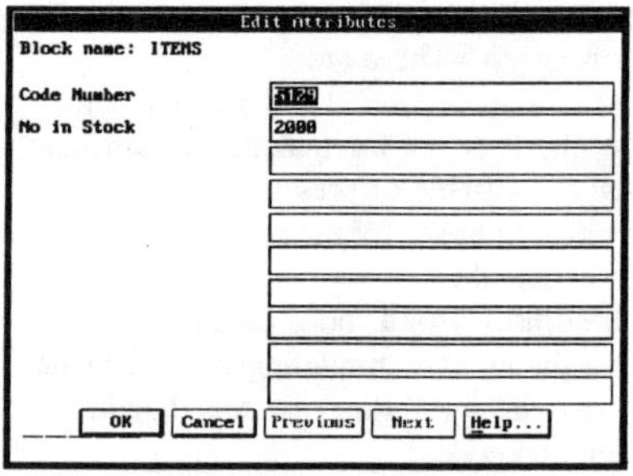

8.4 DDATTE Dialogue Box

DDATTEXT*
- extracts attribute values and stores them

Command Sequence
Command: **DDATTEXT**
→ **UTILITY** → **ATTEXT:** → **Att Ext Dialogue**
↓ **DRAW** → **TEXT** → **ATTRIBUTES** → **EXTRACT...**

Command Options

The action of DDATTEXT is much the same as that of ATTEXT except that a dialogue box is used. A template file must have been set up previously as explained in the description of ATTEXT.

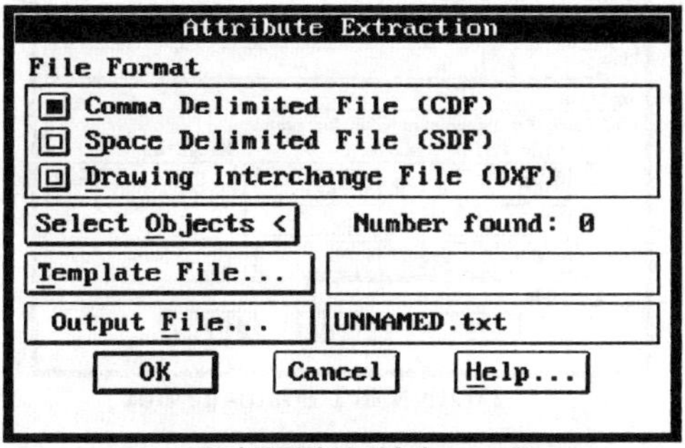

8.5 DDATTEXT Dialogue Box

The dialogue box contains four sections:

- File Format is used to define the way that attribute values are to be stored. The file may be one of three types: CDF, SDF or DXF. Details may be found in the description of ATTEXT.
- Select Objects< enables the selection of the blocks from which attribute values are to be extracted.
- Template File... displays a dialogue box which may be used to search for and specify the required template file. In order to search for the file, a pattern using wild cards may be placed in a Pattern box.
- Output File... is used to nominate the file in which the attribute data is to be stored. This is also done using a secondary dialogue box.

DDINSERT*

- inserts a block into the current drawing

Command Sequence

Command: **DDINSERT**
↓ **DRAW** → **INSERT...**

Command Options

Previously stored Blocks and drawings may be inserted into the current drawing using either INSERT which uses command line options, or DDINSERT which uses a dialogue box. The dialogue box displayed on entering this command contains three main areas: Select Block Name, Options and Explode.

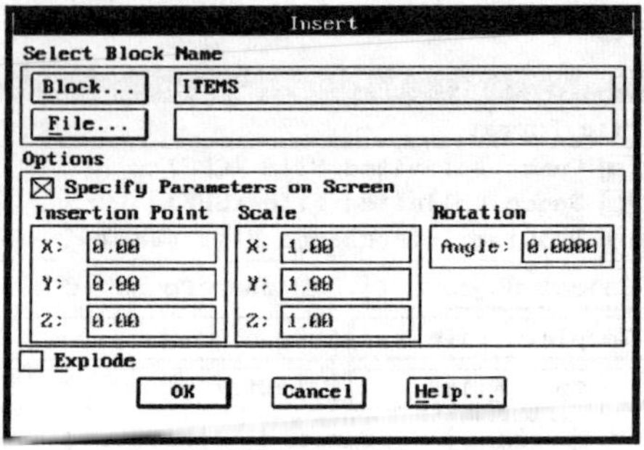

8.6 DDINSERT Dialogue Box

- Select Block Name contains two buttons: Block... and File.... These may be used to specify the name of the block or drawing to be inserted. Clicking on either of these buttons results in the display of a secondary dialogue box which enables a search to be made for previously stored blocks and drawings, possibly with the help of a wild card pattern.
- The Options box is used to control the way that the insertion point is specified. The insertion point coordinates, and the scale and rotation values for the block may be defined on the current drawing. Alternatively, some or all of the values may be defined directly in the dialogue box in the edit boxes provided.
- The Explode check box enables blocks to be inserted in the drawing as their component entities. To do this, the scale values in each coordinate must be equal.

INSERT

- inserts a block into the current drawing

Command Sequence

Command: **INSERT**
→ **DRAW** → **INSERT:**
→ **BLOCKS** → **INSERT:**
↓ **Draw** → **Insert**

Command Options

The user is prompted for the block name by Block name (or ?) <default>:. The default name is that of the last block inserted. If the name provided is prefixed by an asterisk, the block is exploded before being inserted so that the component elements may be edited separately. If the block named has not been defined in the current drawing, a search is made for it in the AutoCAD search path. If it is found, then it is available for insertion. If not, the command is terminated. If, instead of a block, a drawing is to be inserted, a tilde (~) should be entered. This will result in the display of a Select File dialogue box from which the file may be specified conveniently.

Insertion point: is the next prompt. A block has an associated reference point; the insertion point is where this point will be placed on the drawing. The insertion point is also the datum for scaling the block and the pivot for a rotation. The insertion point may be defined by typing coordinates or by dragging the block into position. In the latter case, the block rotations and scale may be defined by entering one or more of the preset commands: Scale, Xscale, Yscale, Zscale or Rotate. After a preset command has been issued, the numeric value must be specified. The Scale preset command scales the block equally in all coordinate directions. Differential scaling may be done by using Xscale, Yscale or Zscale. If the precise scales and rotation are not yet determined, temporary values may be given by prefixing the commands by P. In this case, the values only influence the form of the block as it is being dragged; the actual values must be set later.

If the scale and rotation have not been preset, the prompt X scale factor <1>/Corner/XYZ: appears. The default is a scale factor of one and, in this case, the block is scaled as it was defined.

If the Corner option is taken, the scales may be set by picking a box on the display. If XYZ is chosen, prompts will be issued for the scale factors in each direction. A negative scale factor results in the block being mirrored. If differential scaling has been used, the inserted block cannot subsequently be exploded.

Finally, the rotation angle must be supplied after the prompt Rotation angle <0>:. RETURN results in the block being inserted with no rotation. The desired rotation angle may be input directly or by moving the cursor to a point on the display, the rotation angle then being defined as the angle from that point and the insertion point.

MINSERT
- draws an array of blocks

Command Sequence
Command: **MINSERT**
→ **BLOCKS** → **MINSERT:**
→ **DRAW** → **MINSERT:**

Command Options
This command is a combination of BLOCK, ROTATE and ARRAY, copies of the named block being inserted as a rectangular array which is an entity. The block must first be named in response to the prompt: Block name (or ?):. The ? prompt results in the display of a list of currently defined blocks. If a tilde ("~") is entered, the Select Block dialogue box appears. This shows a list of drawings available for insertion. It is not possible to insert a block in its unexploded form as may be done using INSERT.

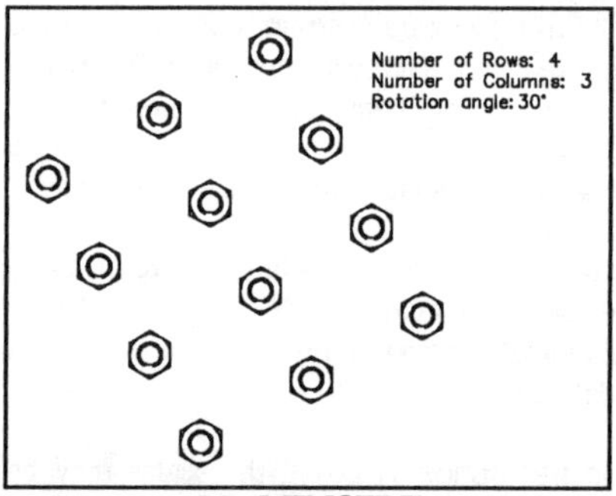

8.7 MINSERT

Next, an insertion point must be specified after the prompt: Insertion Point:. This is followed by definition of the X scale factor, the prompt being X scale factor:, then the Y scale factor after Y scale factor (default = X):. In the latter, if RETURN is typed, the scale factor is taken to be the same as that in the X-direction.

The prompt Rotation angle: permits an angle of rotation about the insertion point to be defined. The number of rows and columns are entered after Number of rows (--): and Number of columns(|||):. The distance between rows may be provided after Unit cell or distance between rows (--):. If this is entered as a numerical value, the system prompts for Distance between columns(|||):. Alternatively, the Unit cell option may be taken. This specifies both row and column distances by defining diagonal corners of a box. The second corner is defined after the prompt Other corner:. A positive distance creates copies of the block in the positive directions - right along the X-axis, up along the Y-axis. If a negative distance is entered, copies of the block will be generated in the opposite directions.

SHAPE
- inserts a shape entity

Command Sequence

Command: **SHAPE**
→ DRAW → next → SHAPE:

Command Options

Shapes are similar to blocks in that they are collections of objects that may be inserted into a drawing. The difference is that the block becomes part of the drawing file. When a shape is inserted, only a reference to it is added to the drawing file, together with its size and insertion point. This means that any change in a shape file will be reflected in a change in the appearance of a drawing in which the shape has been inserted. This type of external referencing may also be done (in Release 12) by using XREF. Before using a shape, its definition file must be compiled from .SHX form to .SHP form using the COMPILE command.

A shape may be inserted after the first prompt: Shape name (or ?):. If the ? option is selected, a list of currently loaded shapes may be obtained before selection. The datum for the shape is defined after the prompt: Starting point:. Height: is the next prompt. The shape's size, defined in the shape file may be adjusted on the drawing by entering a scale factor.

The shape may be rotated on the drawing by specifying an

angle after Rotation angle:. This (and the height) may be provided by pointing.

WBLOCK

- stores a block in a file

Command Sequence

Command: **WBLOCK**

→ **BLOCKS** → **WBLOCK:**

Command Options

The difference between this command and the BLOCK command is that, in WBLOCK the block is saved on a file externally to the drawing database. In BLOCK, the block is only saved in the drawing database. A block saved using WBLOCK may be inserted into subsequent drawings.

The name of the file in which the block is to be stored is provided in response to the prompt: File name:. Blocks are treated like ordinary drawings in AutoCAD so that their default file name extension is DWG. This does not need to be specified; the system adds it automatically. If a file of that name is already stored, the user is asked if the existing file is to be overwritten.

Block name: is the next prompt. If instead of a block name, an equals sign (=) is typed, a block of the same name as the file name is sought in the drawing file. Or, if an asterisk (*) is typed, the whole current drawing is taken as the block. This is a good way of cleaning up the drawing file, since all redundant information will be discarded before the drawing is stored. If RETURN is entered, a set of entities may be selected for storage to the file. In this case, an insertion point must also be provided.

XBIND

- externally binds external drawings to the current drawing

Command Sequence

Command: **XBIND**

→ **BLOCKS** → **XBIND:**

Command Options

External drawings, such as blocks, may be defined in a drawing by using the INSERT and DDINSERT commands. They then become part of the drawing database. A more flexible method is to reference them externally using the XREF command. In this case, blocks are not stored (or bound) in the drawing database; they are cross-referenced.

This has the advantage that the drawing file is smaller. It also has the effect of transferring any change in the block definition to the drawing database without any editing being required. There is, however, a danger that unwanted changes may be made to the block or that it might be erased completely. The XBIND command converts selected elements of an externally referenced drawing to the normally bound form.

A range of possible item (or symbol) types is displayed in the prompt: Block/Dimstyle/LAyer/LType/Style: A selection may be made from this list of the type to be made permanent. The item's name must then be defined in response to the prompt: Dependent symbol name(s): where symbol is the type of item selected. An item selected will have a name in the database of the current drawing. The database is scanned for possible candidates for selection. These are then displayed in the form:

External_reference_name|Named_objects_name

They are then bound to the drawing database.

XREF
- inserts references to external drawings

Command Sequence

Command: **XREF**
→ **BLOCKS** → **XREF**

Command Options

External drawings such as blocks may be defined in a drawing by using the INSERT and DDINSERT commands. They then become part of the drawing database. A more flexible method is to reference them externally using the XREF command. In this case, blocks are not stored (or bound) in the drawing database; they are cross-referenced. This has the advantage that the drawing file is smaller. It also has the effect of transferring any change in the block definition to the drawing database without any editing being required. The XBIND command is the converse of XREF. It converts selected elements of an externally referenced drawing to the normally bound form.

?/Bind/Detach/Path/Reload/<Attach>: is displayed.

- ? displays a list of the external references in the current database. Selected references may be chosen using wild cards.
- Bind makes selected external references permanent in the database. The prompt Xrefs(s) to bind: is given. Several names, separated by commas, may be entered. The references are stored as blocks and are automatically named in a way that will not conflict with any blocks defined in any other way. The format used is:
  External_reference_name$Number$Symbol_name
  The number is incremented at each occurrence of the reference. This option acts like the XBIND command.
- Detach removes an external reference completely from the drawing database. A prompt Xref(s) to detach: is issued and the name of the reference input. Several reference names, separated by commas, may be entered.
- Path is used to re-define the path for finding external references. Selected reference names are input in response to the prompt: Edit path for which Xref(s):. Then the current path name is displayed and the new one entered.
- Reload is used to update an external reference without leaving the drawing editor. This is especially useful in a networking environment when it is known that the cross-referenced is likely to be changed during a drawing session.
- Attach is the default option and is used to insert an external reference. The name of the external reference must be supplied after the prompt: Xref to attach <current XREF name>:. Insertion point: is the next prompt. A reference has an associated datum point; the insertion point is where this point will be placed on the drawing. The insertion point is the datum for scaling the referenced block and the pivot for a rotation. The insertion point may be defined by typing coordinates or

by dragging the block into position. In the latter case, the block rotations and scale may be defined by entering one or more of the preset commands: Scale, Xscale, Yscale, Zscale or Rotate. After a preset command has been issued, the numeric value must be specified. The Scale preset command scales the referenced block equally in all coordinate directions. Differential scaling may be done by using Xscale, Yscale or Zscale. If the precise scales and rotation are not yet determined, temporary values may be given by prefixing the commands by P. In this case, the values only influence the form of the block as it is being dragged; the actual values must be set later.

If the scale and rotation have not been preset, the prompt X scale factor <1>/Corner/XYZ: appears. The default is a scale factor of one and, in this case, the block is scaled as it was first defined. If the Corner option is taken, the scales may be set by picking a box on the display. If XYZ is chosen, prompts will be issued for the scale factors in each direction. A negative scale factor results in the block being mirrored. If differential scaling has been used, the inserted block cannot subsequently be exploded.

Finally, the rotation angle must be supplied after the prompt Rotation angle <0>:. RETURN results in the referenced block being inserted with no rotation. The desired rotation angle may be input directly or by moving the cursor to a point on the display, the rotation angle then being defined as the angle from that point and the insertion point.

APPLOAD
- loads AutoLISP and ADS applications

Command Sequence
Command: **APPLOAD**

Command Options
ADS (AutoCAD Development System) is a C programming language binding system. It allows C programs to work with AutoCAD. These are generally substantial programs; it is easier to write small routines in AutoLISP, the list processing language which comes with standard AutoCAD. The file, APPLOAD.DFS, holds details of ADS programs.

The APPLOAD command can be used to unload ADS programs. In contrast, AutoLISP programs cannot be unloaded.

On issue of the APPLOAD command, the Load AutoLISP and ADS Files dialogue box is displayed. This has the options:

- Files to Load: A list of applications is displayed in the dialogue box. Selections are made for the applications to be loaded or removed.
- File: This option results in the display of a secondary dialogue box: the Select Lisp/ADS Routine box. This is used to add applications to the Files to Load list.
- Remove: Selections made in Files to Load are removed from the list.
- Load: Selections made in Files to Load are loaded.
- Unload: ADS selections made in Files to Load are unloaded.
- Save List: This is a check box. If it is filled in, the APPLOAD.DFS file is updated on selection of Load, Unload or Exit.

The system variable MAXSORT is used to control the sorting of the list of applications in Files to Load.

COMPILE*

- converts shape and font definition files into SHP files

Command Sequence

↓ **File** → **Compile...**

Command Options

A file dialogue box is displayed on receipt of the COMPILE command. This contains a list of SHP (shape) and PFB (Adobe Type 1 font) files. Files for compilation are selected from the list.

DDVIEW*

- creates, deletes and restores views

Command Sequence

Command: **DDVIEW**

→ **DISPLAY** → **VIEW** → **View Dialogue**

↓ **View** → **Set View** → **Named View...**

Command Options

A dialogue box listing the names of the views currently saved is displayed. There are seven buttons: Restore, New..., Delete, Description, and the usual OK, Cancel and Help.

- Restore. If a listed name is selected and the Restore button clicked, the view is restored in the drawing.
- New... When this button is clicked, a secondary dialogue box appears. The name of the new view is entered in the edit box. There are two radio buttons Current Display and Define Window. The first defines the displayed drawing as the view, the second allows a window to be picked on the drawing. The defined view may then be saved by clicking the Saved View button.
- Delete. If a listed view name is selected and this button clicked, that view is deleted.
- Description... Information about the selected view is displayed in the dialogue box which results from clicking the Description button.

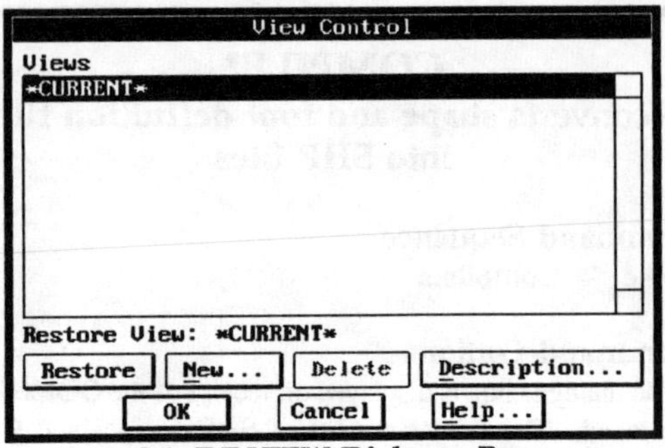

9.1 DDVIEW Dialogue Box

DXBIN
- imports DXBIN files

Command Sequence

Command: **DXBIN**

→ UTILITY → DXF/DXB → DXBIN:

↓ File → Import/Export▸ → DXB In...

Command Options

DXB (Binary Drawing Exchange) files are used to transfer drawing information set up in AutoCAD to other programs such as AutoSHADE. They are not exact definitions of the drawing since curved entities are converted to chains of short straight lines in them. This command imports a DXB file into AutoCAD.

A File Selection dialogue box is displayed, the file name is selected and the file imported when the OK button is clicked.

DXFIN
- imports a DXF file

Command Sequence

Command: **DXFIN**

→ UTILITY → DXF/DXB → DXFIN...

↓ File → Import/Export → DXF In...

Command Options

DXF (or Drawing Interchange) files are used to transfer drawing information between AutoCAD and other CAD systems. Many wordprocessors (eg WordPerfect), Desktop Publishing systems (eg PageMaker) and drawing systems (eg CorelDRAW) can import DXF files.

The DXFIN command imports a DXF file into a current drawing. To prevent any conflict between settings, the current drawing is given preference. So, if the incoming DXF file's layers, blocks, linetypes, linetype scales and text styles are to be transferred, the current drawing must be empty. Normally, entry to the drawing editor calls up the prototype drawing ACAD.DWG but an empty drawing may be obtained by selecting No Prototype in the Create New Drawing dialogue box or by typing the name of the new file followed by an equals sign in the dialogue box displayed after the OPEN command.

A File Selection dialogue box is displayed, the DXF file name is selected and OK clicked.

DXFOUT

- creates a DXF file

Command Sequence

Command: **DXFOUT**
→ **UTILITY** → **DXF/DXB** → **DXFOUT:**
↓ **File** → **Import/Export** → **DXF Out...**

Command Options

The Create DXF File dialogue box is displayed if the system variable FILEDIA is set to 1. A list of currently held DXF files is shown on the dialogue box, the system detecting them by their extension .DXF. One of these files may be selected if it is intended to overwrite it. Or a new filename may be typed - there is no need to add the extension .DXF since AutoCAD does it automatically. If FILEDIA is unset, a new filename must be input on the command line.

A prompt Enter decimal places of accuracy (0 to 16)/Entities/Binary <6>: is issued on clicking OK. If the whole drawing is to be converted to DXF form, it is sufficient to take the six decimal place accuracy default by entering RETURN or typing the number of places required.

If only selected entities are to be stored in DXF form, the Entities option is entered. A Select Objects: prompt results and the required entities selected. The initial prompt will then be re-displayed.

There are two kinds of DXF file - the ASCII and binary types. The ASCII is readable to a user, the binary is not. The binary file is held to the same accuracy as the drawing file. Binary files are smaller and load to AutoCAD faster. If a binary file is required, the Binary option is selected and the file is stored.

FILES*
- performs file operations

Command Sequence
Command: **FILES**
→ UTILITY → FILES:
↓ File → Utilities...

Command Options
If the system variable FILEDIA is set to 1, the commands are issued through a set of dialogue boxes. If FILEDIA is unset, the commands are issued in response to prompts on the command line.

9.2 FILES Dialogue Box

The Files Command dialogue box has six buttons: List files..., Copy file..., Rename file..., Delete file..., Unlock file... and Exit. The Exit button if clicked results in a return to the drawing editor. The other five buttons have associated secondary dialogue boxes.

- List files...A Files List dialogue box is displayed. Initially, the listing pattern is set to *.DWG so that only drawing files are listed. The pattern may be reset, using wildcards, to show any other set of files.

- Copy file...The Source File dialogue box results. The file to copy from is selected from the files list. The Destination File dialogue box is used to define where the copy is to go and what it is to be called. On clicking OK, the file is copied and a return made to the drawing editor. In the case of any problems, a message is displayed at the bottom of the dialogue box.
- Rename files...The Old File Name dialogue box is displayed. The name of the file to be renamed may be selected from the list or typed in explicitly. When the OK button has been clicked, the New File Name dialogue box appears. The new name of the file selected is entered, being either picked from the list or typed directly. On clicking OK, the renaming is carried out. In the case of any problems, a message is displayed at the bottom of the dialogue box.
- Delete files...The File(s) to Delete dialogue box is shown. Files to be removed from storage are selected from the file list. Selected subsets of files may be deleted by typing names in the Pattern box using wildcards. All listed files may be selected for deletion using a Select All button. If a group of files has been chosen mistakenly, a Clear All button is also provided. When OK has been clicked, the number of files successfully deleted is shown as a message at the bottom of the dialogue box. Locked files cannot be deleted. They must first be unlocked.

  If AutoCAD is being used on a network, it could be disastrous for two people to try to edit the same file simultaneously. To avoid this problem, AutoCAD creates a lock file when a file is accessed. If a further access is attempted, the system informs the second user that there is a lock on the file. The lock file may be monitored continually until it is free. Or, the access attempt may be abandoned by typing CTRL-C. If the system has been left untidily, for instance by pressing CTRL-ALT-DEL, the lock file may exist even though no one is trying to access the associated file. The lock file may be removed from the system by using this command. Lock files are easily detected; their extension ends in "K". For example, a locked .DWG file has a lock file with an extension .DWK.
- Unlock file...The Files to Unlock dialogue box appears. The names of the files to unlock are selected using the file list or typing a pattern possibly using wildcards. An attempt is made to unlock the specified files when

OK is clicked, the system reporting progress at the bottom of the dialogue box.

If the system variable FILEDIA is unset (set to 0), each of the items in the dialogue boxes has its counterpart in an option shown on the command line.

GIFIN*/TIFIN*
- imports a raster image

Command Sequence
Command: **GIFIN** or **TIFIN**

Command Options
GIF (Graphics Interchange Format) and TIF (Tagged Image File) are popular formats for raster images. On input, a raster image file is converted into an AutoCAD block. Files produced this way can be very large so these commands (and PCXIN) must be used with discretion. Probably the best way to proceed is to import a raster file, trace it using normal AutoCAD entities, then delete the underlying block. This is a useful procedure since it is an efficient way of transferring a scanned image to an AutoCAD drawing. Scanners usually produce output in GIF or TIF form.

The options are straightforward. The file name is input, then the prompt Insertion point <0,0,0>: requires the block insertion point to be specified. X, Y, Z coordinates may be typed, an insertion point may be picked or the default taken by entering RETURN.

The block may then be scaled with the insertion point as datum by defining a scale after the prompt: Scale Factor:. This can be done by entering a numeric scale factor or using the cursor. If RETURN is entered, the scale factor may be specified by picking a point.

There are six settings which may be used to control the appearance of the block in AutoCAD.

- RIASPECT controls the aspect ratio of the raster image. This is defined as a real number.
- RIBACKG sets the background colour of the image.

- RIEDGE controls the degree of boundary detection which will be performed on the raster image. 0 disables boundary detection; a value of from 1 to 255 sets how stringent will be the boundary detection. 1 will import most detail, 255 will omit features of the image which are not very well defined. This is useful if the raster image is to be traced and is most effective if a line drawing has been scanned.
- RIGAMUT determines the number of colours used in the imported image. The default is 256 but this can be reduced to match the capability of the display or to reduce the drawing file size.
- RIGREY, if set to a number greater than zero, results in the image being imported in grayscales.
- RITHRESH acts as a filter on the incoming image. The numeric setting acts as a brightness threshold, areas with brightness values less than the setting being ignored.

The successful setting of most of these variables requires experimentation. GRIPBLOCK should be unset (to 0) so that the many entities of a block derived from a raster image will not have grips displayed.

IGESIN/OUT
- imports and exports IGES files

Command Sequence

Command: **IGESIN** or **IGESOUT**
→ **UTILITY** → **IGES** → **IGESIN:** or **IGESOUT:**
↓ **File** → **Import/Export▸** → **IGES In** or **IGES Out**

Command Options.

The IGES (Initial Graphics Exchange Specification) format is probably the most widely used for exchanging drawings between different drafting systems. If the system variable FILEDIA is set to 1 then either the Select IGES File dialogue box or the Create IGES File dialogue box is displayed depending on whether the command issued was IGESIN or IGESOUT.

- The Select IGES File dialogue box shows a list of currently stored IGES files from which a selection may be made. These have an extension of .IGS.
- The Create IGES File box shows the current drawing

name. This name may be used for the IGES file or a new one typed after pressing the Type it button.

- The OK button initiates the loading or storing of the IGES file.
- There is in both boxes a button called Default. This resets the dialogue box back to default settings.

If FILEDIA is unset, prompts equivalent to those in the dialogue box will appear on the command line.

LOAD
- loads a compiled shape definition file

Command Sequence
Command: **LOAD**
→ DRAW → next → SHAPE: → LOAD:

Command Options
If FILEDIA is set to 1, a Select Shape File dialogue is displayed. This lists all currently available shape files which the system detects by their extension of .SHX. When a shape file is selected from the list, and the shape it defines will become available for use with the SHAPE command.

If FILEDIA is unset, prompts equivalent to those in the dialogue box will appear on the command line.

NEW*
- starts a new drawing

Command Sequence
Command: **NEW**
↓ File → New...

Command Options
Before the new drawing is started, a box appears allowing changes to the current drawing to be saved or discarded. Also, opportunity is given for the NEW command to be cancelled. If it is not cancelled, the Create New Drawing dialogue box is displayed. The name of the new drawing may be entered in the box on the upper right hand side of the dialogue box. There are also four options governing the

loading of a prototype drawing:

- Prototype.... If this button is clicked, the Prototype Drawing dialogue box appears. This shows a list from which a prototype may be selected. The list includes the default prototype drawing ACAD.DWG. The new drawing will contain all the entities and the settings of the prototype drawing. This is commonly used as a tool for standardising drawings.
- No prototype. This box, if clicked, results in the default AutoCAD settings being used in the new drawing.
- Retain as Default. If this box is checked, the selected prototype drawing will be kept as the default for new drawings.
- New Drawing Name.... The Create Drawing File dialogue box is displayed if this button is clicked. A path name for the new drawing may be entered. The new drawing filename and the prototype drawing name may be entered together, the new drawing filename being typed first, then an equals sign, then the prototype drawing name. If no name is entered after the equals sign, the new drawing will be started with no prototype.

OPEN*

- loads a drawing into the drawing editor

Command Sequence

↓ File → Open...

Command Options

The OPEN command results in the display of the Open Drawing dialogue box. This box contains a list of currently available drawings which the system detects by their extension of .DWG. A drawing may be selected from this list by clicking on its name. If it is wished to change the directory or disk drive, then this may be done by selection from the file list. A box displays the Pattern used to compose the list. This may also be used to display a list of a subset of the drawings stored by using wildcards. Or the box: Type it may be clicked so that the filename may be entered directly. Other buttons in the dialogue box are: Select Initial View and Read Only Mode.

- Select Initial View, if chosen, produces a secondary dialogue box which enables a view defined in the selected drawing to be shown on loading.

- Read Only Mode is a check box which disables storage of changes in the selected drawing.

PCXIN*
- imports a PCX raster file

Command Sequence
Command: **PCXIN**

Command Options
The prompt: PCX file name: is displayed and the filename typed.

Subsequent operations are precisely the same as are described for the command GIFIN.

PLOT*
- produces a plot on a configured plotter or a plot file

Command Sequence
Command: **PLOT**
→ **PLOT...**
↓ **File → Plot...**

Command Options
In AutoCAD releases previous to Release 12, plotting was controlled from prompts on the command line. This can stil be done if the system variable CMDDIA is set to 0. Otherwise, a detailed dialogue box, the Plot Configuration box, is displayed. Using this has many advantages, possibly the greatest being that plots may be previewed.

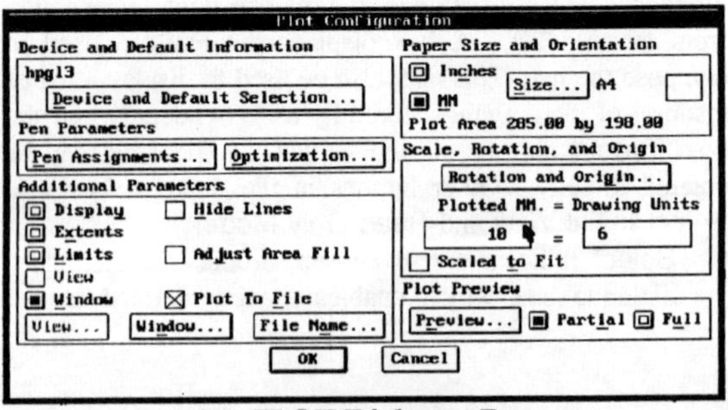

9.3 PLOT Dialogue Box

The Plot Configuration dialogue box is divided into five partitions.

- Device and Default Information. This button permits a selection to be made from a long list of plotters and printer-plotters using the Device and Default Selection dialogue box. Previous to using the command PLOT, devices used by the system have been chosen using the CONFIG command. One of these may be chosen from the list displayed. It is a common practice to include plotters which are not physically available. The drawings can then be plotted to a file which may be used for transfer between sites or for import to other systems. The settings chosen in the Plot Configuration box may be stored in a plot configuration file (extension .PCP). Using this facility, several plot configurations may be selected and loaded using the Get Default from File button. Show Device Requirements (if active) displays information about the plotting device. Change Device Requirements enables plotter configuration data to be set. This is device dependent.
- Pen Parameters. This box contains two buttons. The Pen Assignments... button is used to map AutoCAD colours to plotter pen numbers. Other plotter characteristics may be set here. These will depend on the capabilities of the selected plotter; they may include parameters such as pen speed and plotter linetypes. The Optimization button is used to produce a secondary dialogue box on which may be specified the levels of plotter pen optimisation which AutoCAD will carry out. These include pen sorting, so that all the operations carried out by a given pen are completed before another pen is selected and endpoint swap, which means that a series of parallel will be drawn from different directions in alternate passes of the pen. The more intelligent plotters can automatically optimise plots and electrostatic plotters are becoming more popular. In either of these cases, it is better to disable optimisation.
- Paper Size and Orientation box has two radio buttons: Inches and MM. These are used to define the units when paper size is set. If the Size button is clicked, the plot paper may be set to any size consistent with the currently selected plotter. The plot may be oriented in either landscape (normal for plots) or portrait aspect ratios.
- The Scale, Rotation, and Origin box has just one

button. This is called Rotation and Origin. Clicking on it results in a dialogue box: Plot, Rotation and Origin. The plot may be rotated by a angle selected from 0, 90, 180 or 360 degrees. The plot origin may be set to desired values.

- The final set of options is contained in the Plot Preview box. Two types of preview may be obtained: Partial or Full. The Partial option results in a preview showing the plot sheet with a rectangle round the plotted drawing. The Full option results in a diagram of the plot sheet with the plotted drawing detailed on it.

PSDRAG*

- controls the appearance of PostScript images on input

Command Sequence

Command: **PSDRAG**

Command Options

The way command PSIN operates is influenced by this command. PSIN drag mode <0>: is the only prompt returned. If 0 is entered, only boundary lines surrounding the PostScript drawing will be shown while it is being dragged. If PSIN drag mode is set to 1, the PostScript file will be interpreted and the image shown.

PSFILL*

- provides PostScript area fills

Command Sequence

Command: **PSFILL**

Command Options

This command fills areas contained within polyline boundaries. The first prompt is Select polyline: after which the boundary for filling is picked. The pattern name is then typed after Postscript fill pattern (. = none) <.>/?:. A list of patterns available may be obtained by typing ?. If the pattern name is preceded by an asterisk, the bounding outline will not be printed.

PSIN*
- imports an EPS (Encapsulated PostScript) file

Command Sequence
Command: **PSIN**

Command Options
The filename is supplied in response to the prompt: File:. Next, the bottom left hand corner of the imported file is positioned by supplying an insertion point after the prompt: Insertion <0,0>:. Finally, if required, the image may be scaled after Scale factor:.

When the file is loaded, a box enclosing it is displayed. This may be dragged into position. When it has been placed, it is turned into an AutoCAD block. The PostScript version is stored with the AutoCAD data so that the file may be exported using the command: PSOUT.

PSOUT*
- exports a drawing as an EPS (Encapsulated PostScript) file

Command Sequence
Command: **PSOUT**
→ **UTILITY** → **PSOUT:**
↓ **File** → **Import/Export** → **PostScript Out**

Command Options
Many desktop publishing and other programs accept input in PostScript form. The most general way to control the output of PostScript drawings is by means of the file ACAD.PSF. This can be edited to give different options for the conversion to the EPS file. Probably the easiest item to control is text. A PostScript font may be mapped to a standard AutoCAD font and substituted for it in the EPS file by editing a section *fonts in ACAD.PSF. Since PostScript is a language in its own right, it is probably best not to tamper with ACAD.PSF unless the elements of the language are known.

The command PSOUT results in the Create PostScript File dialogue box being displayed. Using this a new filename may be created or an existing file overwritten by the EPS version of the drawing. The remaining options permit various sections of the current drawing to be selected for conversion to EPS.

The sections selectable are:

- Display. All the visible drawing area.
- Extents. The bounding area of all the defined entities.
- Limits. The drawing bounded by the currently set LIMITS.
- View. The area defined by an existing view which has been defined previously.
- Window. An area selected by picking a window with the cursor

A screen preview image may also be included in the file. The type of image (None/EPSI/TIFF) may be defined followed by the size of image (128/256/512 pixels square).

PSQUALITY*

- sets the quality of images imported by PSIN

Command Sequence

Command: **PSQUALITY**

Command Options

There is only one prompt issued after the command PSQUALITY. This is New value for PSQUALITY<75>: after which a number in the range -75 to 75 may be returned. The absolute value of the number input determines the quality of the imported file; it is the number of pixels which will be mapped to one drawing unit. If a negative number is input, no area fill will be carried out. If zero is chosen, only a box bounding the image will be displayed.

QSAVE*

- saves the current drawing immediately

Command Sequence

Command: **QSAVE**

↓ **File → Save**

Command Options

This command should be issued frequently throughout a drawing session. The current drawing, if named, is saved without further user intervention. If it is still nameless, the Save Drawing As dialogue box is displayed and the drawing can be named.

RCONFIG

- reconfigures the display and hard-copy devices for rendered images

Command Sequence

Command: **RCONFIG**

↓ **Render → Preferences → Reconfigure**

Command Options

After the RCONFIG command has been issued, the display flips to the text screen. The configuration menu for the current rendering device is shown and options may be chosen from the four displayed.

- Option 0. Exit to drawing editor. The configuration changes may be changed or discarded before exit.
- Option 1. Show current configuration. This option displays the current configuration settings.
- Option 2. Configure rendering device. The display may be reconfigured to support the rendering required. Current settings are shown.
- Option 3. Configure hard copy rendering device. The device may be reconfigured to support the rendering required. Current settings are shown.

SAVE

- saves the current drawing

Command Sequence

Command: **SAVE**

→ **SAVE:**

↓ **File → Save**

Command Options

After the SAVE command has been issued and if the system variable FILEDIA is set to 1, the Save Drawing As dialogue box is displayed. This has a list of files with possibly a scroll-bar if the number of files is too large to fit in the space allocated for the list. Apart from the standard OK, Cancel and Help... buttons, there are Type It and Default buttons. There are also text boxes for file Pattern and File:. If the current drawing has been given a name, that name is entered in the File: box. When the current drawing is saved, the previous version is backed-up to a file with extension .BAK and with the same name as the original.

The default shows all the files with the extension .DWG. since the pattern is set to *.DWG. The list may be altered by navigating the disk using the directory change facilities in the list- eg \ (Backslash) for the root directory and .. (double dot) for the parent directory. Drives may also be changed.

New patterns may be set in the Pattern: box using wildcards. The Type it: button allows the filename to be entered at the Command: prompt; the Default button returns the dialogue box to its default condition. In this state, the Default button is grayed out.

When the file has been identified and selected satisfactorily, clicking OK saves it. If FILEDIA is unset (with value 0), the options are displayed successively on the command line. They are equivalent to those present on the dialogue box.

SAVEAS*

- saves a drawing under a fresh name

Command Sequence

Command: **SAVEAS**
↓ **File → Save as...**

Command Options

This command works in the same way as SAVE except that a new file name is required.

SAVEIMG

- saves the current drawing in GIF, RND, TGA or TIFF format

Command Sequence

Command: **SAVEIMG**
→ **RENDER → SAVEIMG**
↓ **Render → Files → Save Image**

Command Options

There are three items which must be defined: the image name, the graphics format to be used and the portion of the image which has to be saved. To set these, a dialogue box, the Save Image box is displayed.

The image name may be typed in the Image Name box.

The type of file, whether GIF, RND, TGA or TIFF should be picked through the radio buttons in the Format: box. There are sub-options available for TGA and TIFF files. These can be uncompressed (and quickly loaded) or compressed (and slowly loaded). The compression method used may be chosen to be one of two alternatives in the case of TIFF.

The part of the drawing to be saved is set by using one of three radio buttons in the Portion box. These may be used to save: the Active viewport, the Drawing area or the Full screen. If the rendering device is configured to give full screen rendering, the portion can be picked by windowing.

The edit box at the bottom of the box displays the coordinates of the bottom left corner of the image to be saved. The size box displays the distance (in pixels) from bottom left of the image to its top right. Both of these may be edited.

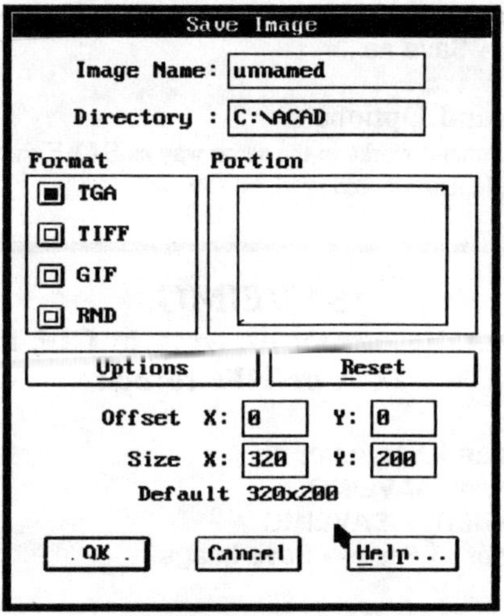

9.4 SAVEIMG Dialogue Box

10 The Drawing Environment

ABOUT

- displays the AutoCAD logo and general information

Command Sequence

Command: **ABOUT**
→ **UTILITY** → **next** → **ABOUT:**
↓ **File** → **About AutoCAD**
'ABOUT

Command Options

This command has no options. It displays information such as the release number, serial number and names of licensee and vendor.

CONFIG*

- configures AutoCAD devices

Command Sequence

Command: **CONFIG**
↓ **File** → **Configure**

Command Options

The current configuration setup is displayed. Configuration parameters may then be changed after selecting numbered options from a menu. The AutoCAD supported devices are displayed, a selection made and parameters set. Available configuration options are:

- 0. Exit to drawing editor. Changes may be either saved or discarded before exit.
- 1. Show current configuration. A list of current settings is displayed.
- 2. Allow detailed configuration. This enables options following to be performed in greater detail.

- 3. Configure video display.
- 4. Configure digitizer.
- 5. Configure plotter. Release 12 treats plotters and printer plotters in exactly the same way so, commonly, more than one device is configured.
- 6. Configure system console.
- 7. Configure operating parameters. This allows various parameters to be set. It produces a list of options:

  0. Exit to configuration menu
  1. Alarm on error
  2. Initial drawing setup
  3. Default plot file name
  4. Plot spooler directory
  5. Placement of temporary files
  6. Network node name
  7. Automatic-save features
  8. Full-time CRC validation
  9. Automatic Audit after IGESIN, DXFIN or DXBIN
  10. Select Release 11 hidden line removal algorithm
  11. Login name
  12. Server authorization and file-locking

DDEMODES

- sets colour, elevation, linetype, text style and thickness

Command Sequence

Command: **DDEMODES**

→ **SETTINGS** → **DDEMODES**

↓ **Settings** → **Entity Modes...**

Command Options

The command produces the Entity Creation Modes dialogue box. This box provides the options that can be set using the commands: COLOR, DDLMODES, ELEV, LINETYPE, STYLE. Secondary dialogue boxes are displayed when the corresponding buttons are clicked.

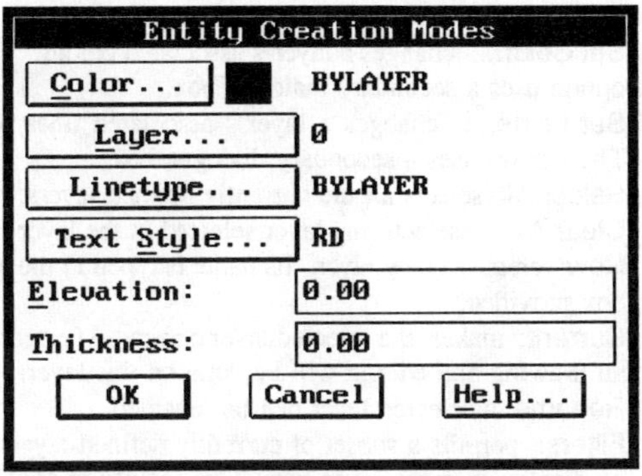

10.1 Entity Creation Modes Dialogue Box

DDLMODES

- controls layers

Command Sequence

Command: **DDLMODES**

→ **LAYER...**

↓ **Settings** → **Layer Control...**

Command Options

The Layer Control dialogue box is displayed. This contains a list of the current layers and their associated names, states, colours and linetypes. Layers may be selected from the list and selected layers are highlighted. A bank of buttons is also provided, permitting settings of selected layers to be made.

- On/Off: turns layers on or off.
- Thaw: changes layers from the Frozen state to the Thawed state. Thawed layers are available for turning on.
- Freeze: changes layers to the Frozen state.
- Unlock: removes the lock from layers so that entities on them may be edited.
- Lock: prevents any change to layers.
- Cur VP Thw: thaws layers in current viewport. This, like the next three options, only affects paper-space entities.
- Cur VP Frz: freezes layers in current viewport.
- New VP Thw: thaws layers in new viewports.

- New VP Frz: freezes layers in new viewports.
- Set Color...: changes a layer's associated colour. This option uses a secondary dialogue box.
- Set Ltype...: changes a layer's associated linetype. This option uses a secondary dialogue box.
- Select All: selects all the currently defined layers.
- Clear All: deselects any layer selected in the layer list.
- New: creates a new layer. Its name is typed in the edit box provided.
- Current: makes the selected layer current. Afterwards, all drawing and editing will be done on this layer.
- Rename: a selected layer can be renamed.
- Filters: permits a subset of currently defined layers to be displayed in the layer list. This facility is enabled and disabled using a button labelled On. There is another button, Set..., which produces the Set Layer Filters dialogue box. This may be used to list layers only with selected attributes.

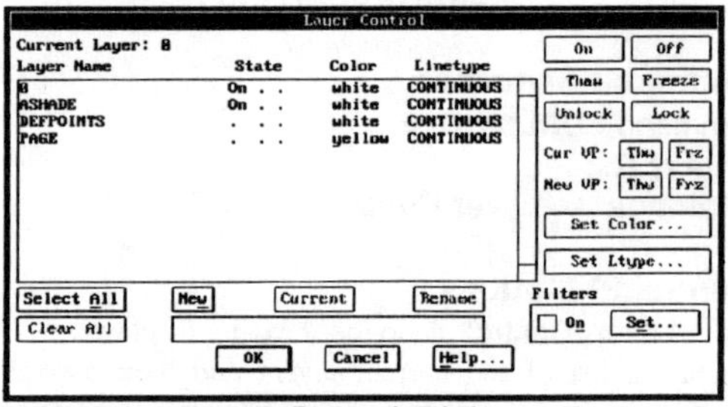

10.2 Layer Control Dialogue Box

DDOSNAP*

- sets object snaps

Command Sequence

Command: **DDOSNAP**

↓ **Settings → Object Snap**

'DDOSNAP

Command Options

Object snaps are set through the Running Object Snap dialogue box. This contains check boxes for each type of object snap, details of which may be found in the description of the OSNAP command:

- Endpoint
- Midpoint
- Center
- Node
- Quadrant
- Intersection
- Insertion
- Perpendicular
- Tangent
- Nearest
- Quick

A slider bar is also provided for setting the aperture size of the osnap pick box.

The command OSNAP may also be used to set object snap modes. It does not use a dialogue box. The system variable OSMODE holds the value of the object snap combination currently in force. The system variable APERTURE holds the pick box height in pixels.

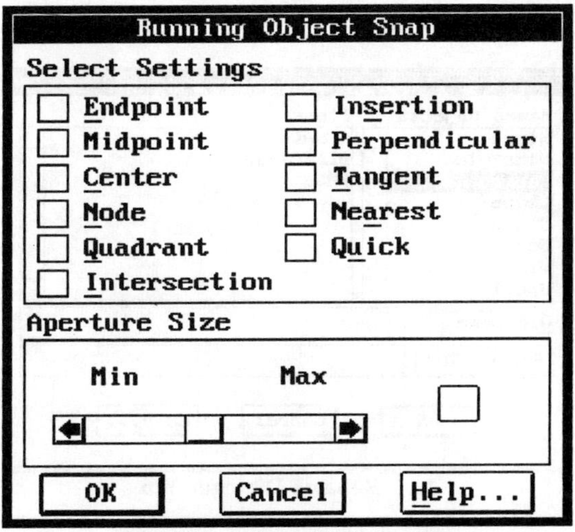

10.3 Object Snap Dialogue Box

DDRENAME*

- renames any nameable object

Command Sequence

Command: **DDRENAME**

→ Utility → Rename: → Rename Dialogue

Command Options

Objects which can be renamed using DDRENAME are blocks, dimension styles, layers, linetypes, text styles, UCS settings, views and viewport settings.

The Rename dialogue box is displayed. On the left there is a list of things that can have names. On the right there is space for a list of the objects that have been given names in the current drawing. To use this, the type of object is selected from the box on the left, all currently named objects of that type are displayed in the box on the right.

To rename one of the objects, it is first selected from the list shown in the box. Its name appears in a space called Old Name:. The new name is typed in a box beneath called Rename To:. Wild cards may be used to rename groups of objects.

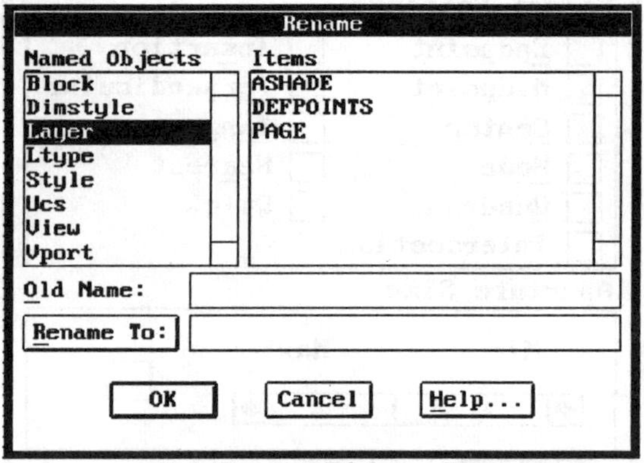

10.4 Rename Dialogue Box

DDRMODES

- sets and unsets various drawing aids and modes

Command Sequence

Command: **DDRMODES**

→ **SETTINGS** → **DDRMODES**

↓ **Settings** → **Drawing Aids...**

'DDRMODES

Command Options

The Drawing Aids dialogue box is displayed. This has toggles for:

- Ortho: enabling or disabling orthogonal snaps.
- Solid Fill: controls whether the system variable FILL is ON or OFF. If it is ON, subsequent wide polylines, traces and solids will be filled.
- Quick Text: text is shown by the bounding rectangle if Quick Text is ON.
- Blips: blips are drawn if toggled ON.
- Highlight: selected items are highlighted.

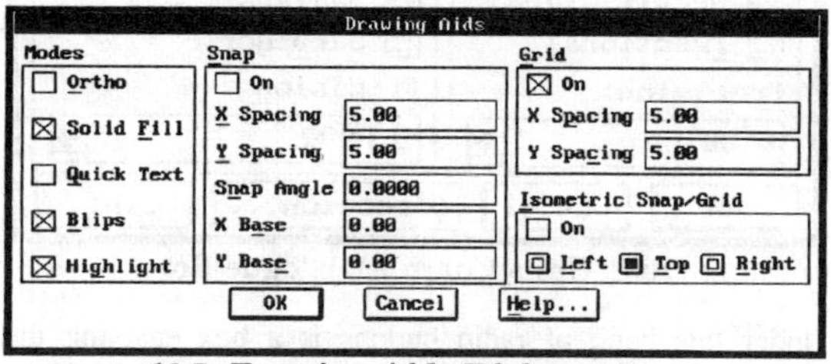

10.5 Drawing Aids Dialogue Box

It has a section for toggling Snap ON or OFF. This also contains areas in which may be set the snap X and Y spacing, the snap angle and the coordinates of the snap base.

Another group is concerned with grid settings. The grid can be toggled ON and OFF, and the grid spacing set in the X and Y directions. The Isometric snap grid also has a group. The Isometric mode may be toggled ON and OFF and the isometric working plane selected from the three available.

DDUNITS*

- controls units and number formats

Command Sequence

Command: **DDUNITS**

→ SETTINGS → next → UNITS: → DDUNITS

↓ Settings → Units Control...

Command Options

In the Units Control dialogue box, there is a set of radio buttons for selecting the units to be used. These are:

- Scientific: eg 1.45E+01
- Decimal: eg 14.50
- Engineering: eg 1'-2.50"
- Architectural: eg 1'-2 1/2"
- Fractional: eg 14 1/2

10.6 Units Control Dialogue Box

Under this bank of radio buttons is a box enabling the precision to be set. The number of digits to the right of the decimal place may be specified.

Another set of radio buttons enables the format for angular measurement to be defined:

- Decimal Degrees: eg 45.0000
- Degrees/mins/secs: eg 45d0'00"
- Grads: eg 50.0000g
- Radians: eg 0.7854r
- Surveyor's units: eg N 45d0'0" E

Under this set of radio buttons is a box in which angular precision may be set.

At the bottom of the dialogue box is a button labelled: Direction. If this is clicked, a Direction Control dialogue box appears. This is used to set the datum and positive direction for angular measurement. The datum angle may be set using radio buttons to East, North, West, South or any other direction entered as an angle. The positive direction may be set to either Clockwise or Counter-Clockwise.

END

- saves the current drawing and exits the drawing editor

Command Sequence

Command: **END**

→ **UTILITY** → **next** → **END:**

Command Options

There are no options for this command.

FILTER*

- enables the creation of object filters

Command Sequence

Command: **FILTER**

→ **EDIT** → **next** → **SELECT:** → **Filters**

↓ **Assist** → **Object Filters**

'FILTER

Command Options

FILTER is used to set up complex selection sets. The command is normally used in two places; at the Command: prompt, to set up selection sets for subsequent commands and transparently during a Select Objects: sequence. FILTER sets up a list of properties which must be possessed by objects which are candidates for selection.

The Entity Selection Filters dialogue box is displayed.

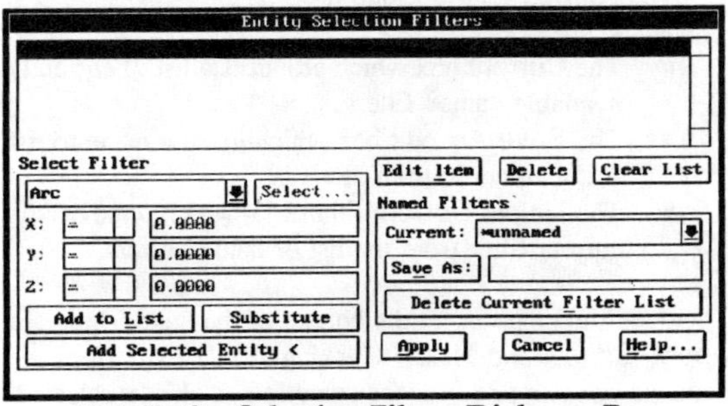

10.7 Entity Selection Filters Dialogue Box

This has three option groups in which filters are set up. When this has been done, the Apply button at the bottom of the box is clicked and the filters are then in force for subsequent selections which are made after the prompt Select Objects:

The Entity Selection Filter List Box has a list of currently selected filters. In order to operate on the list, three buttons are provided:

- Edit Item permits highlighted items in the list to be copied to the Select Filter group for editing
- Delete removes highlighted items from the list
- Clear List removes all items from the list

- The Select Filter group has:
    - a scrollable list box of all the types of filter available.
    - a button Select... which, when clicked, results in the display of a dialogue box showing all the kinds of object with which the filter type can be associated.
    - the X, Y and Z options displaying the relational operators available in those coordinate directions. These are equal to (=), not equal to (!=), greater than (>), greater than or equal to (<=), less than (<), less than or equal to (<=).
    - The Add to List button adds the current filter setting to the Filter List.
    - The Substitute button replaces the filter selected in the Filter List with the current filter setting.
    - Add Selected Entity< inserts the properties of a selected entity to the Filter List.
- The Named Filters group has:
    - The Current box which produces a list of currently available named filters.
    - The Save As: edit box which gives a name to the set of filters in the Filter List.
    - The Delete Current Filter List which removes the current filter from the list of named filters.

There are three buttons at the bottom of the box. These are Apply, Cancel and Help. Clicking Apply exits from the dialogue box and performs the operation on objects selected.

GRID

- creates a grid of points, used as a drawing aid with snap

Command Sequence

Command: **GRID**
→ **SETTINGS** → **GRID:**

Command Options

Grid spacing (X) or ON/OFF/Snap/Aspect <0.0000>: is displayed. If a number is entered, the grid spacing will be set to that number of drawing units. If the number is followed by X, the grid spacing will be set to that number multiplied by the current snap setting.

- ON/OFF enables or disables the display of the grid. If the grid spacing is too small to be displayed, a message will be issued. The grid may be toggled on and off at any time by using either Ctrl-G or F7.
- Snap sets the grid spacing to the current snap setting.
- Aspect permits the grid to have different spacings in X and Y directions. The X and Y values in drawing units are entered in response to prompts.

The system variables GRIDMODE and GRIDUNIT are set by this command. GRIDMODE is set to ON if the grid is displayed; GRIDUNIT holds the spacing values.

HANDLES

- enables or disables the provision of handles

Command Sequence

Command: **HANDLES**
→ **SETTINGS** → **HANDLES:**

Command Options

Handles are entity identifiers which are stored in the drawing database. They may be used to reference entities by programs external to AutoCAD.

The prompt is ON/DESTROY:. If DESTROY is chosen, handles are removed from current and subsequently defined entities. This action is so drastic that safeguards are provided. Unlike other prompts, the whole keyword must be typed. Also, a warning message is displayed together with a keyword, randomly chosen from a defined set. This must be typed correctly in order for handles to be destroyed.

The system variable HANDLES is set to 1 if handles are on and 0 if handles are off.

LAYER

- creates and controls layers

Command Sequence

Command: **LAYER**

Command Options

The main prompt is: ?/Make/Set/New/ON/OFF/Color/ Ltype/Freeze/Thaw/Lock/Unlock:

- ?: lists all layers defined in the current drawing.
- Make: creates a new layer and sets it as the current layer. The name of the layer is entered and subsequent entities are drawn on that layer until another layer is made current.
- Set: makes current a previously defined layer.
- New: creates one or more new layers. The names are separated by commas and may be up to 31 characters long.
- ON: turns layers on. Wild cards may be used to turn on groups of layers. Layers which are turned on are visible on the screen.
- OFF: turns layers off. Although a layer which is turned off is not visible on the display, its entities are considered during regeneration. The current layer may be off.
- Color: allocates a colour to a layer. Entities drawn on that layer are drawn in the allocated colour if their colour is set to BYLAYER.
- Ltype: allocates a linetype to a layer. Entities drawn on that layer are drawn in the allocated linetype if their linetype is set to BYLAYER.
- Freeze: turns layers off so that they are not displayed

but they are also ignored during regeneration. This is a useful facility to reduce regeneration time while developing large drawings. A frozen layer may be turned on and will be then displayed but will still be ignored during regeneration.

- Thaw: unfreezes layers. They may, after unfreezing, be turned on. They will then take part in regenerations.
- Lock: prevents any changes to layers.
- Unlock: allows entities on layers to be added and edited.

AutoCAD supports an unlimited number of layers. There are two special layers created by the system. These are Layers 0 and DEFPOINTS. DEFPOINTS is used to carry the points used to create an associative dimension. Entities may not be drawn on the DEFPOINTS layer. Layer 0 has white continuous lines. It is the default layer on entry to the system. If a block is created on Layer 0, and if its colour or linetype have been set BYLAYER, the block will, when inserted on another layer, assume the properties of that layer.

LIMITS

- defines the drawing boundary

Command Sequence

Command: **LIMITS**
→ SETTINGS → LIMITS:
↓ SETTINGS → Drawing Limits

Command Options

LIMITS is used to define the corners of a rectangle within which drawing must be done. The limits only apply to X and Y directions; there are no limits in the Z direction. The limits are only notional - limit checking may be turned off if desired. There may be different limit settings in Modelspace and Paperspace.

The first prompt issued is: ON/OFF/<Lower left corner>:. ON enables and OFF disables limit checking. If limit checking is ON, any attempt to draw outside the limit boundary will result in a warning message. The default option requires the specification of the bottom left corner of the limit box. This may be entered in coordinate form. Entering RETURN results in the default coordinates being taken. These are often <0.00,0.00> unless they have been set up differently in the prototype drawing.

Next, the top right corner must be specified in response to Upper Right Corner:. Again, RETURN results in the top right corner set in the prototype drawing being defined.

The limits set are referred to in other commands. In ZOOM, the ALL option may result in the screen showing the drawing's limits or extent, whichever is larger. And in PLOT, the limits of a drawing may be plotted.

When the system variable GRID is turned ON, the grid is displayed as a rectangle covering the drawing's limits.

MULTIPLE

- enables a command to be performed repeatedly

Command Sequence

Command: **MULTIPLE** (followed by the command to be repeated).

Command Options

The command following MULTIPLE is repeated until Ctrl-C is input. MULTIPLE may be used with all commands except END, PLOT and QUIT.

MVSETUP

- sets up the drawing layout

Command Sequence

Command: **MVSETUP**

↓ View → Layout → MV Setup

Command Options

MVSETUP may be run in two ways: in pre-Release 12 mode or in Release 12 mode. On entry of the command, Enable Paper/Modelspace? <Y> is displayed. If N is returned, then the pre-Release 12 mode will be in force. This only provides a small number of the wide range of facilities offered by the Release 12 version. In this case (or if TILEMODE is set to 1), the prompts which follow are:

> Select the units from the screen menu:
> Select the Scale from the screen menu:
> Select the Paper size from the screen menu:

Only these three operations are available. Units may be selected from a list identical with that shown after the UNITS command. In the next option, a scale may be typed or may be selected from a list showing the common scales used. Similarly, a list of standard paper sizes is offered in the next option. A choice may be made from this, or a paper size defined by typing its width and height.

If Y is chosen, in response to the first prompt, or if TILEMODE is set to 0, the Paperspace setup is started. This provides facilities for creating, scaling and aligning viewports in Paperspace and also of adding a title block to the drawing. The prompt is Align viewports/Create/Scale viewports/Options/Titleblock/Undo:.

- Align viewports: allows a view to be rotated in a viewport and viewports to be aligned horizontally and vertically using a basepoint and an alignment point on the view in the viewport.
- Create: allows various viewport layouts to be set up. Possible arrangements are:
  - Single: one viewport whose extents are specified.
  - Std. Engineering: four views in a specified area. These are usually: top view, front elevation, right elevation and isometric view.
  - Array of viewports: a rectangular array of viewports.

  This option also permits objects to be deleted from a viewport.
- Scale viewports: allows all or some viewports to be scaled. The ratio between Paperspace and Modelspace is set numerically.
- Options: selects or creates the layer on which the title block is to be placed. Limits may be set automatically to the size of the title block. Paperspace units - feet, inches, millimeters etc - may be selected. Also, the title block may be inserted as a normal block defined in the drawing file or may be defined as an external reference.
- Title Block: determines the form and placement of the

title block. Objects may be deleted from the drawing. An origin point may be defined. One from a displayed list of available title blocks may be selected and drawn. The list of title blocks may be added to and blocks deleted from the list. Title blocks may be converted into drawings.

- Undo: acts just like the normal UNDO command. Previously performed operations may be annulled.

ORTHO
- constrains picked points orthogonally

Command Sequence
Command: **ORTHO**
→ SETTINGS → ORTHO
'ORTHO
Ctrl-O
F8

Command Options
ORTHO constrains a subsequently picked point so that it is at a relative angle of 0 or 90 degrees from the previously defined point.

The prompt ON/OFF: is issued. ON sets the system variable ORTHOMODE and displays the reminder ORTHO on the status bar. If the point is defined by coordinates rather than by picking, ORTHO is ignored. ORTHOMODE may also be set using the DDRMODES command. If the drawing is in isometric mode, it is assumed that the orthogonal constraint is on the current isoplane.

OSNAP
- selects one or more object snaps

Command Sequence
Command: **OSNAP**
→ * * * *
→ SETTINGS → next → OSNAP:
↓ Assist → Object Snap
'OSNAP

Command Options

The prompt Object snap modes: is given.

One or more choices may be made from the twelve possible modes. Only the mode's first three letters need be typed.

- CENter snaps to the centre of an arc or circle.
- ENDpoint snaps to the closest end of a line or arc.
- INSert snaps to the insertion point of text, blocks, attributes or shapes.
- INTersec snaps to the nearest intersection point of two entities.
- MIDpoint snaps to the middle point of a line or arc.
- NEArest snaps to a point on an entity nearest to the pick point.
- NODe snaps to a point.
- PERpend snaps to a point on a line, arc or circle that is perpendicular to the last point defined.
- QUAdrant snaps to the nearest quadrant point on an arc or circle.
- QUIck snaps to the first point found which satisfies all the object snap modes currently set. It is only used with other modes.
- TANgent snaps to the point on an arc or circle that, when connected to the last point defined, forms a tangent.
- NONe turns off object snap.

Each object snap mode is allocated a numeric code which is a power of two. The current object snap combination is held in the system variable OSMODE as the sum of the number codes.

The system variable APERTURE holds the object snap aperture square size. Object snaps may also be set inside drawing commands by typing in the names of the snaps required. When used in this way, the setting only holds for the one point selected. This is known as Object Snap Override.

The command DDOSNAP may also be used to set object snaps using a dialogue box.

QUIT

- leaves the drawing editor without saving the drawing

Command Sequence

Command: **QUIT**
→ **UTILITY** → **next** → **QUIT:**
↓ **File** → **Exit AutoCAD**

Command Options

Prior to Release 12, the question "Really want to discard all changes to drawing?" was displayed. This could be answered by Yes (or Y) or No (or N). In Release 12, a dialogue box appears. This has three buttons: Save Changes, Discard Changes, Cancel Command. This is an added precaution against losing a session's work.

REDEFINE

- restores an AutoCAD command to its default meaning

Command Sequence

Command: **REDEFINE**

Command Options

This command undoes the change to a command made by UNDEFINE. The command to be redefined must be input in response to the prompt Command name:. It will then be restored to its AutoCAD meaning.

Undefined commands may be used in an AutoCAD sense without redefining them if they are entered with a leading full stop.

REINIT*

- reinitialises peripherals

Command Sequence

Command: **REINIT**
→ **UTILITY** → **next** → **REINIT:**

Command Options

The Re-initialization dialogue box is displayed. This has two groups: I/O Port Initialization and Device & File Initialization.

- The I/O Port Initialization group contains check boxes for initialising the ports allocated to the digitiser and plotter during AutoCAD configuration.
- The Device & File Initialization group has check boxes for initialising the digitiser and the display. There is also a check box for reloading the ACAD.PGP file. This is the program parameters file which defines external commands which can be used inside AutoCAD.

RENAME
- changes the names of nameable objects

Command Sequence

Command: **RENAME**
→ **UTILITY** → **RENAME:**

Command Options

Objects that may be renamed are: blocks, dimension styles, layers, linetypes, text styles, UCS settings, views and viewports. The type of object is selected in response to the prompt:
Block/Dimstyle/LAyer/LType/Style/Ucs/VIew/VPort:.
The old and new names are then input. Renaming may also be done using the DDRENAME command which uses a dialogue box.

SETVAR
- lists and changes the values held by system variables

Command Sequence

Command: **SETVAR**
→ **SETTINGS** → **next** → **SETVAR:**
→ ★★★★ → **SETVAR:**
'SETVAR

Command Options

The prompt: Variable name or ?: appears. If the ? option

is chosen, a list of system variables and their current settings is displayed after the prompt: Variable(s) to list <*>:. Wild cards may be used if a subset is required. Many of the AutoCAD system variables are organised in a way that makes this possible. For instance, all dimension system variables start with "DIM". If a variable name is entered, the new value must then be supplied after the prompt: New value for ... <current value>:.

Many system variables may be altered in value by typing their name at the command prompt. The new value may then be entered. The value depends on the type of variable; possible values are integers, real numbers, coordinates and strings. A complete list of Release 12 system variables may be found in Section 12; some of these are read-only and cannot be changed by SETVAR.

SNAP

- controls snap mode

Command Sequence

Command: **SNAP**
→ SETTINGS → next → SNAP:
↓ Settings → Drawing Aids
'SNAP (Release 12 only)
Ctrl-B
F9

Command Options

A snap grid is an array of points. The pointing device may be constrained to point only to the points in the grid. The prompt gives options of turning the snap facility on and off, setting snap spacing, rotating the snap grid and setting isometric snap. When snap is on, the note SNAP is displayed in the status bar. The options are displayed:

Snap spacing or ON/OFF/Aspect/Rotate/Style<1.000>:.

- The default option is to set the snap spacing. This may be done by typing a number or by picking two points. This gives the same spacing in both X and Y directions. If different spacings are needed, then the Aspect option is chosen and the X and Y spacings input.
- The ON and OFF options determine whether snap is on or not. If snap is OFF, the crosshairs may range freely over the display. If snap is turned on, the crosshairs are

positionally constrained to the snap grid.

- The snap grid may be rotated, if the Rotate option is chosen. A pivot point for the rotation is defined in response to the prompt: Base point:. Then the angle of rotation must be defined by either entering the angle as a number or by picking a point. The Style option may be used to convert the standard rectangular snap grid to an isometric grid.

SNAP affects several system variables. These are:

- SNAPANG holds the rotation angle.
- SNAPBASE holds the coordinates of the basepoint.
- SNAPISOPAIR defines the current isoplane.
- SNAPMODE shows whether snap is on or off.
- SNAPSTYL shows whether snap is isometric or not.
- SNAPUNIT holds snap spacing.

TABLET
- sets up input from a digitising tablet

Command Sequence

Command: **TABLET**
→ **SETTINGS** → **next** → **TABLET:**

Command Options

An option is selected from Option (ON/OFF/CAL/CFG):. ON turns on digitised input; OFF returns to normal pointing operation. CAL enables the digitiser to be calibrated with the drawing to be digitised. CFG allows the digitiser to be configured with pointing areas.

- If CAL is selected, points are picked on the drawing, which has previously been secured to the tablet. The calibration may be done in either paper or model space. Either two, three or four calibrating points may be used. Calibration using two points is called Orthogonal. This is sufficient for most purposes. Calibration using three points requires an Affine transformation. It is used when drawings are of unequal scales in two directions.

  If a perspective drawing is to be digitised, four points should be used. The system then carries out a

Projective transformation. When the required number of points have been entered - signalled by entering RETURN - the type of transformation is selected from the options in the prompt: Select transformation type... Orthogonal/Affine/Projective/<Repeat table>:. The Repeat table describes whether the transformation required is physically possible with the points digitised.

- If CFG is chosen, all or part of the tablet surface may be defined as a pointing area. The default menu uses four areas for AutoCAD commands. If the tablet menu to be used has less, the number may be specified in response to the prompt: Enter number of tablet menus desired (0-4) <4>:. If the default is chosen, the four areas may be relocated. If so, the upper left, lower left and lower right corners of each menu area must be picked. The numbers of rows and columns for each area are entered.

  Finally, the part of the tablet reserved for drawing is defined by its lower left and upper right corners. The tablet is then configured. Tablets are discussed further in Section 1.

The areas of the configured tablet may be allocated to specific commands by editing the file ACAD.MNU.

UNDEFINE

- disables an AutoCAD command so that it may be replaced with an ADS or AutoLISP program of the same name

Command Sequence

Command: **UNDEFINE**

Command Options

The name of the command to be undefined is entered at the prompt: Command name:.

The original command may still be used if its name is prefixed by a full stop. Undefined commands may be reinstated by the command REDEFINE.

UNITS
- controls units and number formats

Command Sequence
Command: **UNITS**
→ **SETTINGS** → **next** → **UNITS:**
'UNITS (Release 12 only)

Command Options
The command UNITS performs the same function as the DDUNITS command but uses command line prompts instead of a dialogue box.

Options permit the following to be set:

- Units Formats eg Feet and Inches.
- Number of decimal places.
- Angular Units eg Radians.
- Direction and datum for positive angles.

In detail, the command operates like DDUNITS.

VIEWRES
- sets the resolution of displayed circles and controls fast zooms

Command Sequence
Command: **VIEWRES**
→ **DISPLAY** → **VIEWRES:**

Command Options
The prompt Do you want fast zooms? <Y>: is displayed. If the N option is chosen, each Zoom, Pan or View Restore is accompanied by a regeneration. If Y is chosen, then a large virtual screen will be kept and an attempt made to perform Zoom, Pan or Restore View without regeneration. This means that the operation will be carried out at redraw speed.

A curve, such as an arc, is displayed as a chain of straight line segments. The number of segments is a compromise between appearance and speed of drawing. When a normal zoom is performed, an optimal number of segments is chosen during regeneration to make the curve seem reasonably smooth. When a fast zoom-in is performed and regeneration has not been necessary, the number of segments is not optimised and so may appear more noticeable.

The prompt: Enter circle zoom percent (1-20000)<100>: allows the number of line segments to be controlled. For instance, a circle zoom percent of 200 would permit a zoom of 2X and still allow circles and arcs to be shown optimally. The circle zoom percent also affects linetypes.

VPLAYER
- sets freeze or thaw status of layers within viewports

Command Sequence
Command: **VPLAYER**
→ **MVIEW** → **VPLAYER:**
↓ **View** → **Mview** → **Vplayer**

Command Options
When multiple viewports are being used, it is often necessary to use various layers to control what is being shown in each. The VPLAYER command allows the layer status of viewports to be managed. The prompt: ?/Freeze/Thaw/Reset/Newfrz/Vpvisdflt: is displayed on entry of the command.

- ?: lists the layers and their states for a selected viewport.
- Freeze: freezes one or more layers in the current viewport, all viewports or a selection of viewports.
- Thaw: changes the status of of frozen layers in the current viewport, in all viewports or in a selection of the viewports available.
- Reset: returns to the default status for selected layers.
- Newfrz: creates a set of new layers that are to be frozen in all viewports.
- Vpvisdflt: sets the default visibility for specified layers.

11 Miscellaneous Commands

AREA
- finds areas and lengths

Command Sequence
Command: **AREA**
→ **INQUIRY** → **AREA:**
↓ **Assist** → **Area**

Command Options
AREA can calculate: the area and perimeter of a closed entity such as a circle; the length of an open entity, such as a straight line; the area and perimeter of the figure bounded by a set of points.

The prompt: <First point>/Entity/Add/Subtract: is issued. If a point is selected, the prompt: Next point: appears. A set of points may be picked successively, RETURN ending the sequence. Points must be picked in the order in which they occur around the boundary.

If the option Entity is selected, a circle, polygon or polyline must be picked. Either of these option defines the boundary of the area to be found. If an open polyline is picked, the length of the line joining the first and last vertices will be returned.

The options Add and Subtract may be used to repeatedly add or to subtract areas found by defining boundaries using the point or entity options. A running total is kept of calculated areas. If Subtract is in force, the area is considered to be negative. Neither Add nor Subtract are Boolean operations; the common parts of two overlapping boundaries will be considered twice in the running total.

The results of the calculation are held in system variables AREA and PERIMETER.

AUDIT

- checks for and corrects errors in the drawing database

Command Sequence

Command: **AUDIT**

→ **UTILITY** → **AUDIT:**

Command Options

The command results in an integrity check on the drawing database, which may have become corrupted due to hard or floppy disk malfunction. Before this is done, the prompt Fix any errors detected? <N>: is displayed. If the default option N is chosen, a report showing any errors is generated. If Y is chosen, an attempt is made to correct errors. This may not be successful.

Another command for correcting errors in the database is RECOVER. There is also Task 9 (Recover Damaged Drawing) in the main menu of releases prior to 12.

CAL*

- provides an on-line geometry calculator

Command Sequence

Command: **CAL**

↓ **Assist** → **Calculator**

'CAL

Command Options

Prior to Release 12, an AutoLisp program called CALC was available. This acted as an ordinary calculator. The Release 12 CAL is much more useful, since points may be picked using object snaps and their coordinates used in calculation. CAL provides most of the osnaps defined in the command OSNAP:

- CEN
- END
- INS
- INT
- MID
- NEA
- NOD
- QUA
- PER
- TAN
- RAD
- CUR

These have the meanings described in OSNAP and DDOSNAP except for NOD which stands for NODe, RAD, which returns the radius of a picked object, and CUR which enables unconstrained cursor pick.

Parentheses are used as in ordinary arithmetic. Coordinates are input in square brackets. Arithmetic may be done on either scalars or vectors. Functions and operators provided are:

- Normal arithmetic operators.
- Trigonometric functions and their inverses.
- Rounding operators round and trunc.
- Angular conversion between degrees and radians.
- Vector calculation functions.
- The constant π.

DBLIST

- reports on all entities in a drawing

Command Sequence

Command: **DBLIST**
→ **INQUIRY** → **DBLIST:**

Command Options

The display flips to the text screen and a list of entities, their properties and the layers on which they are drawn is displayed. For any substantial drawing, this scrolls so quickly that it is impossible to read. It is usual to print the list. This is done by hitting the print toggle key Ctrl-Q before using the command.

DELAY

- inserts a delay into a script file

Command Options

The DELAY command is used as part of a script file. It is used with a following number which represents the approximate delay in milliseconds. The maximum number is 32,767.

DIST

- gives the distance between two points

Command Sequence

Command: **DIST**
→ INQUIRY → DIST:
↓ Assist → Inquiry▸ → Distance
'DIST (Release 12 only)

Command Options

DIST prompts for two points and, when these have been entered, returns the distance between them. It also calculates the X, Y and Z components of the line joining the points. The projected angle that the line makes in the XY plane and the angle to it from the XY plane are also returned.

FILMROLL

- creates a file for export to AutoShade or 3D Studio

Command Sequence

Command: **FILMROLL**
→ RENDER → RMAN → FILMROL:
↓ File → Import/Export▸ → Filmroll

Command Options

The file name must be provided. The extension .FLM is automatically added. If the system variable FILEDIA is ON, a dialogue box will appear and the file name may be entered in the edit box. Otherwise, the file name is typed on the command line.

The file contains sufficient information about the three-dimensional objects, surface finishes, view, lights and camera to enable a fully rendered picture to be produced in AutoShade or 3D Studio.

HELP

- provides on-line explanations of AutoCAD commands

Command Sequence

Command: **HELP**
Command: **?**
→ **INQUIRY** → **HELP**
→ ★★★★ → **HELP**
↓ **Assist** → **Help!**
'HELP

Command Options

The Help dialogue box is displayed.

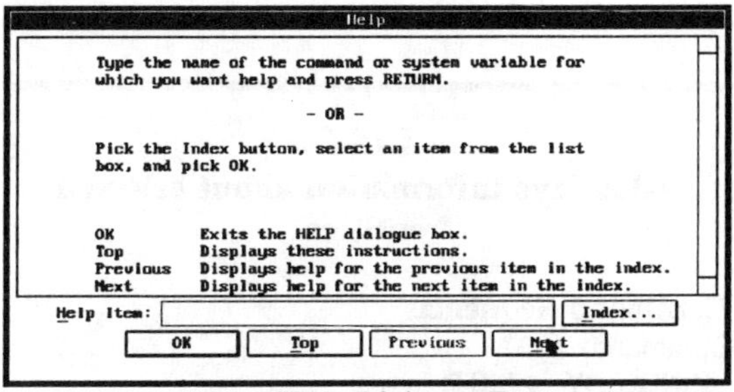

11.1 HELP Dialogue Box

This can contain either an alphabetically ordered list of topics or an explanation of a particular topic. A button Index..., if clicked, produces a list, from which a selection can be made. Or the name of a topic can be entered in an edit box called Help Item: which produces an explanation of that topic.

Button Top displays a list of commands and system variables. Buttons Previous and Next enable information to be paged up and down.

If transparent help is used, by typing 'HELP inside another command, information is displayed about that command.

ID

- returns the X, Y and Z coordinates of a point

Command Sequence

Command: **ID**
→ **INQUIRY** → **ID:**
↓ **Assist** → **Inquiry▸** → **ID Point**
'ID (Release 12 only)

Command Options.

The point is selected in response to the prompt Point: and its X, Y and Z absolute coordinates are returned.

The coordinates of the point selected are held in the system variable LASTPOINT.

LIST

- displays information about selected entities

Command Sequence

Command: **LIST**
→ **INQUIRY** → **LIST:**
↓ **Utility** → **List**

Command Options

The objects to be listed are selected in response to the prompt: Select objects:. The display flips to the text screen and a list of useful information about the selected entity is displayed.

The information shown depends on the type of entity but always includes its type and location, the layer to which it belongs and whether it is in Paperspace or Modelspace.

The information may scroll too fast to be read.. A print-out may be obtained if Ctrl-Q, the print toggle, is hit before entry to the command.

MSLIDE
- creates a slide file

Command Sequence
Command: **MSLIDE**
→ UTILITY → SLIDES → next → next → MSLIDE:

Command Options
A slide is a file which contains a "snapshot" of the display. It contains no structure and the drawing database cannot be reconstructed from it. Slides can be rapidly displayed. A satisfactory drawing should be displayed before the slide is made. On issue of the command MSLIDE, a filename must be provided. This will be automatically given an extension .SLD.

In Modelspace, slides contain only the entities displayed on the current viewport. In Paperspace, the entities displayed in all viewports will be written to the slide. If the system variable FILEDIA is 0, the filename will be entered on the command line. If FILEDIA is set to 1, a File dialogue box will be used.

PURGE
- cleans up the drawing database

Command Sequence
Command: **PURGE**
→ UTILITY → PURGE:

Command Options
PURGE removes from the drawing database any unused blocks, dimension styles, layers, linetypes, shapes and text styles. This command can be used only before any entities have been added to or deleted from the database. If it is wished to purge references on a drawing after it has been edited, the drawing file must be saved and reloaded before purging.

The first prompt to be issued is:

Purge unusedBlocks/Dimstyles/LAyers/
LTypes/SHapes/All:

Either just one type of object or all objects may be selected. As each unreferenced object is found in the database, its name is reported and the user asked whether the object should be purged. Purging may reduce the size of a drawing file so that it takes up less storage space and loads quicker.

A major restriction on its use is that it only removes one level of reference. Any nested definitions, such as blocks, may have to be purged repeatedly by loading the drawing and issuing the command until a message is received that there are no unreferenced objects in the database.

RESUME

- resumes the operation of a script file after it has been stopped

Command Sequence

Command: **RESUME**
'RESUME

Command Options

If Ctrl-C or BACKSPACE are hit while a script is running, the script is interrupted so that normal commands may be issued. The script may be restarted from the place where it was interrupted by using the RESUME command.

RSCRIPT

- makes a script repeat from the beginning

Command Options

The command is used only within a script file. The script file repeats until it is halted by Ctrl-C or BACKSPACE. The command is useful for presentations and demonstrations where it is desirable to play the script over and over.

SCRIPT
- plays a script from within the drawing editor

Command Sequence
Command: **SCRIPT**
→ **UTILITY** → **SCRIPT:**
'SCRIPT (Release 12 only)

Command Options
Scripts are prepared in ASCII characters using a text editor. They contain AutoCAD commands and option selections which can then be run inside the drawing editor. They have many uses, one of the most popular being to make plotting drawings more convenient.

There are some commands which may only be used inside scripts. These are:

- DELAY to pause the script for a fixed time,
- RESUME to carry on with an interrupted script,
- RSCRIPT to repeat the script indefinitely.

The system variable EXPERT is useful in scripts. If its value is 4 or more, then all prompts will be suppressed. The option may then be selected using its name.

Scripts are saved using the extension .SCR. A script may be invoked immediately on entry to AutoCAD by using the construction:

ACAD Drawname Scriptfl

On the command SCRIPT, if FILEDIA is set to 0, the script file name must be input in response to Script file:. No extension is needed. The script file will then be run. If, instead of a name, a tilde (~) is typed, a dialogue box will be displayed.

In the dialogue box, options exist to browse through directories, to enter groups of file names using wild cards and to type a script file name.

SHELL/SH
- switches temporarily to the operating system

Command Sequence

Command: **SHELL** or **SH**
→ **UTILITY** → **External Commands** → **SHELL:**

Command Options

The display is flipped to the text screen and the prompt OS Command: appears. After one DOS command has been executed, a return is made to the drawing editor. Or, RETURN may be typed and the DOS prompt appears allowing more than one DOS command to be executed. In this case, the drawing editor is re-entered by typing EXIT at the DOS prompt.

SHELL requires AutoCAD to free some of its memory for itself and the utility programs that it can run. If insufficient memory is available, an error message is displayed. If only internal DOS commands, such as DIR, are to be executed, then SH is appropriate. This takes far less memory.

Care must be taken not to affect the working environment of AutoCAD by deleting files with extensions of ac$, $a, $ac or ??K. Other potentially disastrous operations are running Terminate and Stay Resident (TSR) programs and running graphics programs that use the same video memory as AutoCAD. It is recommended that the drawing should be saved before using SHELL.

STATUS
- provides information about the current drawing

Command Sequence

Command: **STATUS**
→ **INQUIRY** → **STATUS:**
'STATUS (Release 12 only)

Command Options

Details of the current drawing such as the number of

entities, condition of modes such as Snap and Ortho, grid spacing and current layer and linetype are listed and may be paged by pressing RETURN.

A useful feature of this command is that it shows details of memory usage so that safety measures can be taken if the disk is nearly full.

TIME
- provides time information about the current drawing

Command Sequence
Command: **TIME**
→ **INQUIRY** → **TIME:**
'TIME (Release 12 only)

Command Options
The command provides:
- Current time and date,
- Time and date of creation of the current drawing,
- Time and date of last update,
- Total editing time,
- Elapsed time,
- Time of next automatic save.

A prompt: Display/ON/OFF/Reset: is then issued. Display results in the time information being re-displayed. ON, OFF and RESET may be used to control the elapsed timer. Various system variables affect the time information. The most useful is SAVETIME which controls the time between automatic saves.

TREESTAT
- reports on the status of the current drawing's data structure

Command Sequence
Command: **TREESTAT**

Command Options

If a very large drawing is being worked on, performance may be improved if the data structure of the drawing file is tuned. This is possible using the TREESTAT command.

The drawing is structured in tree form, with separate sub-trees for Paperspace - which is an oct-tree - and Modelspace which is a quad-tree. The TREESTAT command shows the number of nodes, the number of entities and other useful statistics for both Paperspace and Modelspace. The system variable TREEDEPTH may be reset to improve performance after the current tree depth has been displayed.

VSLIDE

- displays slide files

Command Sequence

Command: **VSLIDE**

→ **UTILITY** → **SLIDES** → **VSLIDE**

Command Options

The prompt: Slide file: is displayed and the name is typed. If FILEDIA is set to 1, the File dialogue box is displayed and a slide file name picked from those in the File list.

Files may be extracted from slide file libraries. File libraries are files with the extension .SLB that are used to hold several slide files. If the slide libraries name is SLIDELIB.SLB and the slide file to be extracted is SLIDEFIL, the slide file may be referred to as SLIDELIB(SLIDEFIL) in this command.

12 System Variables

(* means Read-only).

Variable	Description
ACADPREFIX	Environment setting.
ACADVER	Version number.
AFLAGS	Attribute mode setting.
ANGBASE	Angle reference line.
ANGDIR	Angle positive direction.
APERTURE	Osnap target height (pixels).
AREA*	Last area calculation.
ATTDIA	Attribute dialogue box.
ATTMODE	Attribute display.
ATTREQ	Prompt for attributes.
AUDITCTL	Audit file creation.
AUNITS	Angular units.
AUPREC	Angular decimal places.
BACKZ*	Distance target to back clip plane.
BLIPMODE	Blips on or off.
CDATE*	Calendar date/time.
CECOLOR	Default colour.
CELTYPE	Default linetype.
CHAMFERA	First chamfer distance.
CHAMFERB	Second chamfer distance.
CIRCLERAD	Default circle radius.
CLAYER	Current layer.
CMDACTIVE*	Command dialogue box active.
CMDDIA	Dialogue boxes on/off.
CMDECHO	AutoLISP command prompts.
CMDNAMES*	Current active command name.
COORDS	Coordinate readout.
CVPORT*	ID number of current viewport.
DATE*	Date and time.
DBMODE*	Drawing modification status.
DIASTAT*	OK or Cancel on last dialogue box.
DISTANCE*	Last distance calculated.
DONUTID	Donut inside diameter.
DONUTOD	Donut outside diameter.
DRAGMODE	Drag off, on, automatic.
DRAGP1	Regen-drag sampling rate.
DRAGP2	Fast drag sampling rate.
DWGCODEPAGE*	Code page of drawing.
DWGNAME*	Drawing name.
DWGPREFIX	Path of current file.
DWGTITLED*	Drawing named.
DWGWRITE*	Read/write status of drawing.
ELEVATION	Current 3D elevation.
ERRNO*	AutoLISP and ADS error codes.
EXPERT	Detail level of prompts.
EXTMAX*	Top-right corner of extents.
EXTMIN*	Bottom-left corner of extents.
FILEDIA	File dialogue box.

FILLETRAD	Fillet radius.
FILLMODE	Fill on or off.
FRONTZ*	Front clip plane.
GRIDMODE	Grid on or off.
GRIDUNIT	Grid spacing.
GRIPBLOCK	Display of grips.
GRIPCOLOR	Colour of non-selected grips.
GRIPHOT	Colour of hot grips.
GRIPS	Grips on or off.
GRIPSIZE	Size of grips in pixels.
HANDLES*	Handles on or off.
HIGHLIGHT	Highlighting of selected objects.
HPANG	Default hatch angle.
HPDOUBLE	Doubled custom hatch angle.
HPNAME	Default hatch pattern name.
HPSCALE	Hatch pattern scale factor.
HPSPACE	Custom harch line space.
INSBASE	Drawing insertion base point.
INSNAME	Default block name.
LASTANG*	Last arc end angle.
LASTPOINT	Last point specified.
LENSLENGTH*	Focal length of lens in perspective.
LIMCHECK	Limit checking on or off.
LIMMAX	Top-right limit.
LIMMIN	Bottom-left limit.
LOGINNAME*	User's log-in name.
LTSCALE	Linetype scale factor.
LUNITS	Units styles.
LUPREC	Units number of decimal places.
MACROTRACE	Debugging tool.
MAXACTVP	Max. number of viewports to regen.
MAXSORT	Max. number of items to sort in dialogue box.
MENUCTL	Side menu changes on control-line prompt.
MENUECHO	Prompts from menu.
MENUNAME*	Current menu file.
MIRRTEXT	Mirroring of text.
MODEMACRO	Display of custom text in status line.
OFFSETDIST	Offset distance.
ORTHOMODE	Ortho on or off.
OSMODE	Current Osnap mode.
PDMODE	Point marker symbol type.
PDSIZE	Point marker symbol size.
PERIMETER*	Last perimeter calculated.
PFACEVMAX*	Max. number of vertices per face.
PICKADD	Selection set mode.
PICKAUTO	Automatic selection window.
PICKBOX	Size of select objects pickbox.
PICKDRAG	Window definition mode.
PICKFIRST	Pick/Select order in command.
PLINEGEN	Polyline linetype mode.
PLINEWID	Default polyline width.
PLOTID	Default plotter description.
PLOTTER	Default plotter ID.
POLYSIDES	Default number of polygon sides.
POPUPS*	Pull-down menus or not.
PSLTSCALE	Paperspace linetype scale.

PSPROLOG	PostScript prologue for output.
PSQUALITY	Image control for PSIN.
QTEXTMODE	Qtext on or off.
REGENMODE	Regenauto on or off.
REINIT	Hardware re-initialisation.
SAVEFILE*	Autosave file name.
SAVENAME*	User file name.
SAVETIME	Time between saves.
SCREENBOXES*	Number of lines in side menu.
SCREENMODE*	Current display mode.
SCREENSIZE*	Current viewport size in pixels.
SHADEDGE	Shading control.
SHPNAME	Default shape name.
SKETCHINC	Sketch record increment.
SKPOLY	Lines or polylines in SKETCH.
SNAPANG	Snap and grid angle.
SNAPBASE	Snap, grid and hatch origin.
SNAPISOPAIR	Isometric plane.
SNAPMODE	Snap on or off.
SORTENTS	Entity sort options.
SPLFRAME	Spline frame control.
SPLINESEGS	Number of line segments per spine patch.
SPLINETYPE	Type of spline.
SURFTAB1	Number of facets in M direction.
SURFTAB2	Number of facets in N direction.
SURFTYPE	Type of smoothing in PEDIT.
SURFU	Surface density in M direction.
SURFV	Surface density in N direction.
SYSCODEPAGE*	System code page in acad.xmf.
TABMODE	Tablet on or off.
TARGET*	Perspective target point.
TDCREATE*	Time/date of file creation.
TDINDWG*	Total edit time.
TDUPDATE*	Time/date of last update.
TDUSRTIMER*	User- elapsed time.
TEMPPREFIX*	Temporary file location.
TEXTEVAL	Text interpretation.
TEXTSIZE	Text height.
TEXTSTYLE	Default text style.
THICKNESS	Default 3D thickness.
TILEMODE	Paperspace and Modelspace.
TRACEWID	Trace width.
TREEDEPTH	Database search depth.
TREEMAX	Limits maximum number of nodes.
UCSFOLLOW	Automatic change to plan in Modelspace.
UCSICON	UCS icon on or off.
UCSNAME*	Name of current UCS.
UCSORG*	Current UCS origin.
UCSXDIR*	X-direction of current UCS.
UCSYDIR*	Y-direction of current UCS.
UNDOCTL	Current state of UNDO.
UNDOMARKS*	Number of marks set by UNDO.
USER1-USER5	User variables 1-5 for integers.
USERR1-USERR5	User variables 1-5 for reals.
USERS1-USERS5	User variables 1-5 for strings.
VIEWCTR*	Centre of current view.

VIEWDIR* Camera viewing direction.
VIEWMODE* View settings for current viewport.
VIEWSIZE* Height of current view.
VIEWTWIST* Twist angle for current viewport.
VISRETAIN Layer settings for XREF.
VSMAX* Top-right corner of virtual display.
VSMIN* Bottom-left corner of virtual display.
WORLDUCS* WCS on or off.
WORLDVIEW DVIEW and VIEWPORT relative to WCS.
XREFCTL XREF log files on or off.

DimensionVariables.

DIMALT Alternate units off or on.
DIMALTD Alternate units decimal places.
DIMALTF Alternate units scale factor.
DIMAPOST* Alternate units suffix to text.
DIMASO Associative dimensions on or off.
DIMASZ Arrow size.
DIMBLK* Alternate arrow block name.
DIMBLK1* Alternate arrow block name for DIMSAH.
DIMBLK2* Alternate arrow block name for DIMSAH.
DIMCEN Centre mark size.
DIMDLE Dimension line overlap beyond extension line.
DIMDLI Dimmension line offset for base.
DIMEXE Extension line overlap beyond dimension line.
DIMEXO Extension line origin offset.
DIMLFAC Unit scale factor.
DIMLIM Dimension limits on or off.
DIMPOST* Add suffix to dimension text.
DIMRND Rounding value.
DIMSAH Two different arrow heads.
DIMSCALE Overall scale factor.
DIMSE1 First extension line shown or not.
DIMSE2 Second extension line shown or not.
DIMSHO Dynamic update on drag.
DIMSOXD No dimension lines outside extension lines.
DIMTAD Place text above dimension line.
DIMTIH Text inside extensions is horizontal
DIMTIX Text between extensions
DIMTM Minus tolerance.
DIMTOFL Dimension lines between extension lines.
DIMTOH Text outside extension lines is horizontal.
DIMTOL Dimension tolerances.
DIMTP Plus tolerance.
DIMTSZ Tick size.
DIMTVP Tick position.
DIMTXT Text height.
DIMZIN Display of 0 (Zero).